A Long Time Coming

Running Through the Women's Marathon Revolution

By Jacqueline Hansen

Foreword by Joan Benoit Samuelson,
Olympic gold medalist, 1984

Cover photo from 1984 Olympic Trials Marathon
in Olympia, Washington

Jacqueline Hansen was the first woman to break 2:45 in the marathon, then the first to run sub-2:40. Her efforts with the International Runners Committee helped win a spot for this event, and other long-distance races, in the Olympic Games. She now "teaches teachers" at Loyola Marymount University and "coaches coaches" through the LA84 Foundation. This is her first book.

Contents

*Dedicated to the two men in my life who made all
things possible, Laszlo and Tom.*

Foreword

By Joan Benoit Samuelson

With the first Olympic Marathon for women now almost 30 years past, I am sometimes referred to as a "pioneer" for having won that gold medal. I appreciate the thought, but gently point out that I was not one of the pioneers. Instead, our inaugural race in Los Angeles was made possible by the efforts, both physical and political, of earlier women marathoners. They broke down the barriers of intolerance and indifference, starting long before 1984.

At my post-race interviews in Los Angeles, I thanked L.A. Games organizer Peter Ueberroth for his support of my event. I named fellow Olympic marathoners Grete Waitz, Rosa Mota and Ingrid Kristiansen (who became lifelong friends in and outside the sport). I congratulated Gabriele Andersen Schiess for gutting out the race in what could have been a disastrous situation had she not finished, or worse? (Imagine what that would have done for the future of the women's marathon in the Olympics.)

Then I took special care to praise some of the true pioneers by name: Bobbi Gibb, the first woman to finish the Boston Marathon; Sara Mae Berman, the top female there three years in a row; Nina Kuscsik, the first official women's winner at Boston; Miki Gorman, who won both Boston and New York City (twice) after age 40, and of course the author of the book you're now reading, Jacqueline Hansen.

These women of the 1960s and '70s were the heroes, often unsung, of the effort to give us marathoners our rightful place on the Olympic and World Championships programs. With one woman, however, the work didn't stop there. Jacqueline Hansen and the International Runners Committee, which she headed, kept lobbying the officials until women distance runners could run all the same events as men – 5000, 10,000 and steeplechase as well as the marathon.

If the marathon's approval had come sooner, Jacqueline might have been an Olympian herself – maybe even a gold medalist. She set two world records in the 1970s, as the first woman to break 2:45 and 2:40. As it was, her "Olympics" was the 1984 U.S. Trials, when she overcame illness and injury to qualify for that race on the last possible day – then to stand with me and fellow Olympians-to-be Julie Brown and Julie Isphording at the starting line in Olympia, Washington, three weeks later.

How fitting it was that the first Olympic Marathon for women was run in Jacqueline's hometown. And how wonderful that she made me feel at home in L.A. (while arranging housing with my co-hosts, Sherrill Kushner and Ed Kein, right on the marathon course) during my gold-medal Games. Jacqueline has remained a good friend ever since, as well as a great friend of our sport. Her book tells the story of a true pioneer, who has lived the history of our sport and has helped make possible all that we women runners do today.

With Joan at the 2004 Boston Marathon, 20 years after her gold-medal race at the Los Angeles Olympics.

1. They Led Me Here

It won't be long now
Till you drag your feet to slow the circles down
And the seasons, they go 'round and 'round
And the painted ponies go up and down
We're captive on the carousel of time
We can't return, we can only look behind
From where we came
And go 'round and 'round and 'round
In the circle game
And go 'round and 'round and 'round
in the circle game.

Joni Mitchell

In 2012, I had the great honor of being inducted into the U.S. National Distance Running Hall of Fame. This ceremony coincided with the 40th anniversary of Title IX, an act that opened opportunities for women in sports, and would affect girls and women across the nation. I was one of them.

If not for a forward-thinking woman at San Fernando Valley State College, who was a national track and field champion and who became my high school physical education teacher, my life would not have taken the course that it did. Dixie Griffin introduced me to this great sport.

My Hall of Fame induction was a tribute to Coach Griffin and also to my longtime coach, Laszlo Tabori. In 1956 he escaped the Hungarian revolution and the invasion of the Soviets in his home country to compete in the Melbourne Olympic Games. He did not return home. *Sports Illustrated* sponsored many Hungarians, including Laszlo and his coach Mihaly Igloi, who defected to the United States directly from Australia. My fortuitous meeting with Laszlo and more than 20 years of training under his tutelage changed my life forever.

In 2012, I stepped onto the stage for the National Distance Running Hall of Fame induction in Utica, New York, with Larry Rawson of ESPN presenting me. I thanked my hosts, the Hall of Fame Committee, and my friends and relatives who traveled far and wide to be with me. Then I said, "I am glad to have lived the history of women these past four decades, especially through sports. I'm a pre-Title IX baby, a child of the sixties, a feminist of the seventies and a soccer mom of the eighties."

I thanked my predecessors, and it was a long list. Only recently had I learned that America's first woman marathoner had crashed my hometown race, the Western Hemisphere Marathon in Culver City, California. Merry Lepper and Lyn Carman were active in my district and first ran this marathon in 1963. While Lyn did not finish that day, Merry did finish and unexpectedly ran right into history.

Merry helped pave the way for my teammate Cheryl Bridges to run the Western Hemisphere Marathon in world-record time in 1971, as the first woman to break 2:50. Her performance inspired me to run and win my first marathon the following year. Another teammate of mine, Miki Gorman, set the second world record on that same course in 1973, then I followed with the third record set there, in 1974.

In Utica I thanked Merry Lepper on behalf of all of us. In the same era, on the East Coast, Roberta ("Bobbi") Gibb, Nina Kuscsik, Sara Mae Berman, Charlotte Lettis and Kathrine Switzer were all forging the way for women's rights to run in the Boston and New York City Marathons. I'm sure there were even more that I'm not even aware of that deserve mention.

I do know that my part in this history wouldn't have been possible if not for a few coaches early in my adult life. So I am grateful first to my high school coach, Dixie Griffin, who questioned why there wasn't a girls' track team at my school and then created one. She gave me my first chance to be successful at sports, because I was not otherwise very athletic. Her influence on me is that she empowered me to question why – or more importantly, why *not*!

The man who enabled me to become the runner I am is Laszlo Tabori. He trained us all like runners – not female or male runners, just runners. He built an incredibly strong team of women distance runners, including world record-holders and national champions. At the time of my induction Laszlo was traveling to London for the 2012 Olympic Games, to be honored among the world's greatest milers. He was the third man to break four minutes in the mile.

Sadly I could not share my good fortune at the Hall of Fame with my late husband, Tom Sturak, my dear sister Elaine and my good friend Grete Waitz. All three passed away within the previous year. Each one played a significant role in my personal life and my running career. Their absence was and is strongly felt.

Only through the running world did I meet Tom, as I was one of the first women to join his club when Laszlo chose to merge our team with the Southern California Striders. Tom liked to tell the story of how I

10

walked into the first team meeting with an entourage of "Laszlo's boys," me in my mini-skirt and colorful tights, and he said, "I just had to meet you."

Tom was the most liberated male I'd ever met, one who shared my love of running, literature and music. He was fully supportive of my athletic efforts, as I was for his. I'm not sure I would have been so strong throughout the struggle for equality, never mind the struggle of tough workouts and tougher races, had he not been at my side.

My sister Elaine always took good care of me. I credit her for being such an exemplary role model. Even as a young child I was proud to say my sister had an important job in the Air Force, and I was happy that she always brought me exotic dolls from all over the world. She also brought me books whenever she came home, contributing to my becoming a voracious reader from my early childhood until this day.

Later in my adult life Elaine inspired and taught me to cook and bake, even taking me to cooking school for a birthday celebration. I am familiar with the best food writers and love reading their books. Elaine and my sister Nancy have always been my "fan club." I am indeed blessed with such wonderfully supportive people who are the closest to me.

A few women runners served as my heroines. The one I most looked up to in my first club, the Los Angeles Track Club, was Chi Cheng, Olympic medalist (hurdles) and world record-holder from Taiwan. She was the star of the club, and we became good friends. I always remembered her advice to me, to "run like a tiger's chasing you and never look back."

Doris Brown Heritage was another heroine of mine, a pioneer distance runner. She was the world cross-country champion five times. We not only developed a friendship through competing in similar events, but we joined forces in our quest to advance international competition for women distance runners through our work with the International Runners Committee (IRC). Later she mentored me in my first assignment as a U.S. team coach accompanying a squad of women runners overseas. I say proudly that it was Doris who nominated me for the National Distance Running Hall of Fame award.

Then there was Grete, an athlete so renowned that her first name identifies her. To me she was by far the most talented distance runner ever to grace this earth. Beyond that, a good friend called her "without controversy." I call her the most gracious person I have ever met, and I was pleased to call her a friend.

My running career was waning as Grete's was starting, but we shared a few starting lines. When the time came, she generously offered her time as a spokesperson for the cause, the IRC's lawsuit to advance distance events for women in the Olympic Games. She is sorely missed.

These are the folks who influenced me greatly in my early career as a runner. How I came to receive accolades at the National Distance Running Hall of Fame, among other awards, is a story that has been a long time in the making.

With sisters Nancy Boschetti (left of me) and Elaine Ruch (right).

2. "You're No Sprinter"

*To be yourself in a world that is constantly trying
to make you something else is the greatest
accomplishment.*

Ralph Waldo Emerson

My running career had an inauspicious start. But if not
for a fortuitous occurrence in high school my life would
have been quite different. I had struggled with physical
education classes, suffering humiliation at not being
very good at sports, due in part to my short stature. I
also felt rejection as usually I was the last picked for
any game, the perennial bench-warmer. Therefore I
avoided regular P.E. by substituting a variety of elective
classes.

In my senior year of high school, 1966, I took an
elective tennis class and had a chance meeting with
coach Dixie Griffin. A shot putter and javelin thrower
herself, she observed and questioned why there was not
a girls' track and field team, such as the boys
enjoyed. She didn't simply complain against this
inequality; she started the first such girls' team at
Granada Hills High.

Ms. Griffin recruited from her tennis class, and I
volunteered readily to join her track team – partly to be
in good favor for passing the tennis class, and in part to
avoid the spring sport of softball. Besides, out of all the
events in the Presidential Physical Fitness Test that

14

John F. Kennedy had implemented, I only liked the running part.

However, the longest distance girls were allowed to compete in was 440 yards – only a quarter-mile! I may have loved running, but I was no sprinter, and Coach Griffin did not see fit to take me to the city championship meet. Coach Griffin was teased mercilessly for that oversight years later, only to retort that she "always knew Jacqueline was a distance runner."

Indeed my favorite activity as a runner was to see how many laps of the track I could total without stopping. My best friend, Kim Jackson, and I frequently challenged one another this way. My highest total turned out to be 17 laps, four-plus miles, before we had to leave to have our graduation picture taken – me, the one with a red face and track shoes beneath the gown.

This last semester of my last year in high school changed my life in ways I could not have imagined. The two teachers who influenced me most were my English teacher, who inspired a love of literature in a Shakespeare class I shall never forget, and my track coach, for all the obvious reasons.

On Thanksgiving of 2011, the NPR program "Story Corps" encouraged listeners to thank a teacher who was influential in our lives. My thoughts immediately went to these two high school teachers – my English teacher, Paulette Jewell, and my track coach, Dixie Griffin. I've credited both throughout my life, but I must admit I've not tried to contact either one.

Paulette Jewell is the major reason why I became an English literature major in college. She taught in such an engaging manner that she made Shakespeare come alive. I wanted to experience her teaching so much, I took every possible course with her, including a college-credit course on Shakespeare. I was her teacher's assistant when there were no more classes to take. Our final grade in Shakespeare was assessed on our production of the play, "Midsummer Night's Dream," in which I played Helena.

Ms. Jewell, who exemplified what I wanted to become, inspired me to visit the Globe Theater and to frequent Dutton's Bookstore (where the majority of my wish list for high school graduation presents was realized). To this day I love attending "Midsummer Night's Dream" at Topanga's Theatricum Botanicum, the most idyllic setting for this play.

Dixie Griffin's name has come up often when I've done public speaking. The first time I spoke on National Girls and Women in Sports Day, I was retelling my high school experience. A hand was raised and the comment made, "Be careful what you say. You never know who is here." And there Ms. Griffin was in the back of the room. I nearly fell off the podium. It was like that old TV show "This Is Your Life." When I told about how she did not take me to the city meet, she said, "Heck, I knew you were no sprinter."

About five years later I spoke at another National Girls and Women in Sports event, this time at Polytechnic High School in North Hollywood, to an audience of coaches and female athletes. In fact, had my parents not moved from North Hollywood to Granada Hills, Poly would have been my high school. I remember leaving my junior high school friends with tears, feeling it was so unfair to move me to a school where I knew no one. However, as events turned out, it was my good fortune.

So here I was at Poly, giving the same history of my start in track and field, all thanks to a high school P.E. teacher who happened to be an Olympic Trials qualifier

16

in the shot put. The important lesson I learned, as I told my audience, is that Dixie Griffin asked why there wasn't a girls' track team like the boys had, and she created one. As you read the rest of my history, you'll know that this lesson played out well throughout my running life.

It turned out that some of the women coaches attending my talk knew Dixie, and knew that there was a concerted effort in 1966 to expand opportunities for girls in track and field. I investigated further. With the ease of today's Internet search engines, I learned a lot more about Dixie. Here is what my search revealed about her that I never knew before:

In 1956, she was the national champion in the shot put with a record-breaking toss of 37 feet, 10½ inches as a 17-year-old. She went on to the U.S. Olympic Trials, where she did not place in the shot put but was sixth in the javelin throw. Other winners at that meet included Willye White of Tennessee State University in the "running broad jump with a leap of 18 feet, 6 inches; and Wilma Rudolph, also of Tennessee, in the 75-yard dash with a time of 8.3 seconds, as well as the Tennessee [State] 300-yard relay team's winning performance in 32.4 seconds." That's impressive company. Dixie's teammate from the San Fernando Valley, Pamela Kurell, also 17, won the baseball throw, the javelin and the discus.

Far beyond the facts of her competition, I was impressed by an article in the *Los Angeles Times* archives, written in 1959 when Dixie was a student at San Fernando Valley State College. Here are portions of that article written seven years before I met her:

"Is America on the wrong track by not including track and field training for girls? Results of Olympic competition in these events and physical fitness tests among youth, say supporters of their training, show a decline in young women and girls' ability to stack up with other nations. But more important, they add, is their inability to demonstrate strength and coordination that every healthy human should have.

"Points out Dixie Griffin, 20, of Van Nuys, who was national shot put champion… in 1956: 'Running is as basic to physical performance as learning to add is to mathematics. But what girl learns to run correctly?'

"The status quo in American public schools, she said, is not to include any track and field training or competition for girls in the physical education program. If a girl, she continued, wanted to go out for such events, perhaps with her eyes on an Olympic tryouts, she must find an individual coach somewhere who happens to be interested in training her.

"Luckily for her, she said, a physical education teacher at San Fernando Valley State College with a background in these sports taught her how to put the shot and throw the javelin. She and Gloria Griffin [no relation], a sprinter, are among those now working out on the college field in hopes to qualify for the Olympic playoffs.

"What should be done, [Dixie Griffin] and others interested in promoting these sports believe, is to institute track and field for girls in elementary schools, and to have it consistently taught through junior and high school. 'If this is done,' she said, 'U.S. women athletes could compete on a par with other nations at the Olympics on the one end of the scale, and on the other end of the scale, girls would be better developed and more fit from the early training.' "

Wow! Reading this, I am more impressed with Dixie than ever. I knew she impacted my life as an athlete, giving me the opportunity to learn to run. Beyond that, I now realize more than ever how much she influenced me to teach other children how to run.

In testament to her theory, I went on to teach track and field events to children throughout their elementary school years, into middle and high school, simply as a mom of one of those children. A high school coach told me that he loved when the children from my town transferred to his high school. They were well disciplined in our sport. They were like a small and unique lab experiment, having experienced track and field all their school years.

Dixie Griffin was a woman ahead of her time, as her words ring true even today. Perhaps part of the solution to some of the current problems facing our student population could be helped with more physical education rather than cutting it from curriculum.

The same year, 1966, when Dixie gave me the chance to start running, another event would influence the future opportunities for all women to run long distances, me included. Unbeknownst to me then, Bobbi Gibb became the first woman to finish the Boston Marathon (3:21:40). I had never heard of the Boston Marathon at the time.

I was aware of the Olympics, had read the newspapers about Tokyo in 1964 and looked forward to Mexico City in 1968. I couldn't have imagined at the time just how much the marathon and the Olympics would occupy my thoughts and actions in years to come.

My senior photo from Granada Hills High School.

3. Running in College

If a man does not keep pace with his companions,
Perhaps it is because he hears a different drummer.
Let him step to the music which he hears,
however measured or far away.

H. D. Thoreau

I pursued running on the track team when I arrived at Pierce College in the spring of 1968, but without formal training. Our track and field teacher, Ms. Fiorello's, first sport was golf. We learned all the events in an organized and methodical way, as if preparing for skills tests on a weekly basis. My best friend from high school, Kim Jackson, and I now truly relied on each other to see how far we could run on our own after class.

I know we competed as a team, and I have memories of traveling to other community colleges throughout the area, but I do not remember our teacher-coach ever attending those meets with us. It was while traveling with my teammates that I acquired great new R-E-S-P-E-C-T for Aretha Franklin's music. At least the longest race available had increased to 880 yards. I was making progress.

Bob Chambers was the men's coach at Pierce College. I was usually the scorekeeper at all their meets, yet I did not train with them. Sadly we lost two team members on the men's team in that brief time at Pierce, one to a car accident and the other to a sudden

21

heart condition. It was very difficult to cope with these tragedies; we were so young and felt invincible. I remain friends with a few of those team members, and to this day we mourn the loss of those two young men.

It was a violent and tumultuous year, 1968. The assassinations of both Robert Kennedy and Martin Luther King, Jr., had a profound effect – shock, disbelief, hopelessness, despair – as if an extension of the moment in 1963 when John F. Kennedy was killed. His assassination was one of those times in life when you can remember exactly where you were and what you were doing when the news came across the airwaves.

President Kennedy was killed on November 22, 1963, while I was in high school. The news, broadcast through my transistor radio and the public address system at school while we were standing in cafeteria food lines, was shocking beyond belief. Never had anything like that happened in our lifetime. Now, in 1968, such tragedies were repeated again and again. It was unbearable.

The Democratic National Convention in Chicago is remembered for the police and Illinois National Guard clashing with anti-war protesters from a youth movement. Even journalists reporting the event were not immune to violence resulting from what came to be known as the day of the "police riot."

The Mexico Olympics are remembered for the massacre of 43 students just prior to the opening of the Games and the Black Power salute by Tommie Smith and John Carlos on the awards stand for the 200-meter race. (Later I would become friends with Tommie while he was coaching at Santa Monica College and I was at St. Monica High School.)

At that time I could be found most weekends at the Troubadour or other venues seeing and occasionally meeting bands and individuals such as The Byrds, Elton John, Donovan, John Sebastian, John Denver, Peter, Paul & Mary, Eric Clapton, Bob Dylan, Crosby, Stills, Nash & Young, The Who, Jimi Hendrix, James Taylor, Joni Mitchell, Joan Baez, Buffy St. Marie, Cat Stevens, Simon and Garfunkel, Harry Nilsson and Randy Newman. A journal entry describes one such occasion:

My "birthday happening," when Gary and Jeff took me to the Troubadour where we saw John Sebastian. While the show before ours was SRO [standing room only], we got a front row table for the 11 P.M. show and were treated to an added bonus when he brought Donovan up on stage. The audience begged for more, they locked the doors, served more wine and went on for a couple more hours! We even spent time talking with them both after the show. I got home at 4:30 A.M. and had a rough time getting to work the next morning at 7:00. (Note: Gary recently reminded me that they had "let" me purchase wine at a liquor store, telling the clerk it was my 21st birthday after all. True. But neither of them were 21!)

Given that my job, classes and training took over all my waking hours every day, I have a void of knowledge about all television throughout my college years. But I gleaned a great appreciation for all things musical. Much of the music of the times reflected the social and political events in history, like the Kent State shootings memorialized in lyrics, most notably Neil Young's "Ohio."

By the late 1960s, I had transferred from Pierce to San Fernando Valley State College. Valley State was no "Berkeley," but we had our share of controversy and protest. In May 1970 my school was closed down during a strike protesting the Vietnam war.

The overlying backdrop throughout these years was, of course, the war. I still have correspondence from the few friends and one cousin who were sent to Vietnam, and from other friends who were conscientious objectors and stayed behind. The issue of Vietnam permeated every aspect of life in the 1960s and affected everyone.

Again I joined the track team at Valley State, only this time as the only woman. The assigned teacher-coach was a basketball coach who informed me that I could earn my credits by reporting to her weekly and attending the one meet a year, at UCLA. She was satisfied to observe that I was running regularly with some of the guys on the men's team. The longest distance women were allowed to race had now reached one mile.

At home my family had already experienced a difficult year of personal tragedies, including a death and a divorce, when the 1971 Sylmar earthquake seriously damaged our house. Although I was trapped in some rubble when the earthquake struck, for moments that felt like fearsome hours, I only suffered minor cuts and bruises.

Around this time I was introduced to the man who would become my coach. One day, while running loops around a college campus, I happened to meet another woman runner, Judy Graham, and we began to meet regularly for runs. She invited me to meet her coach at a workout at a nearby city college (which we called junior colleges at the time). While competing as a one-woman team at Valley State, attending classes as an English major, and working as much as possible and necessary to support myself, I began training under

Laszlo Tabori. Running soon played a major role in my life, thanks to Laszlo.

Los Angeles Track Club relay team in 1972 (from left): Judy Graham, me, Becky Dennis and Sue Kinsey.

4. Coach Laszlo

Discipline is liberation.
Martha Graham

My chance meeting with Laszlo Tabori began a period
of my life when I learned discipline, dedication and
commitment to a degree I never knew before. Laszlo's
background was intense, and his coaching style was
intense. He was what you could describe as a
disciplinarian-style coach.

I shall never forget my first workout with him. We
ran five big laps around practice fields, about 2½ miles,
followed by 15 times 100-yard "shake-ups" (translated
as wind-sprints) between the goalposts on a football
field inside the track. This was pretty much as far as I'd
ever run at one time in any workout.

The team headed for their track bags, and I thought
we must be done. But no, my Valley State teammate
Jon Sutherland informed me, we were changing into
our racing flats in order to start the hard workout next!

If you ever met Laszlo, you would understand why I
was too intimidated to leave at that point. I was also too
intimidated to stay away the next time and returned for
more of the same the following night. Laszlo had a
commanding presence, to say the least.

Reflecting back, I am very fortunate to have
received the training I did – and in a strange way
fortunate to have progressed in distance running the
way it was imposed. Being limited to quarter-mile

races, then half-mile and finally the mile, my progression was not unlike the English system of developing middle-distance runners as they mature from youth to young adults.

It would seem that I was developed in a pre-planned system of training, what track coaches call "periodization" – except that in my case it was quite unintentional. Perhaps I should call myself an accidental middle-distance runner who became a long-distance runner? It must be unusual to have a collection of medals from the 50-yard dash to the 50-mile run. Honestly!

The fortunate opportunity to train with a man like Laszlo is astonishing when I think of our chance meeting. Naturally he trained us as middle-distance runners because of who he was and how he was coached. When I met him, he had been in the U.S. for more than a decade. Now retired from running, he coached the L.A. Valley College cross-country team.

Laszlo's story is historical. He was a protégé of the famous Hungarian coach, Mihaly Igloi, a man some call the "father of interval training." His runners broke world records from 1000 to 10,000 meters. In 1955 alone, the Hungarian runners broke nine world records and included three of the fastest 1500-meter men in history. Laszlo was the third man in the world to break four minutes in the mile, after Roger Bannister and John Landy.

The Hungarian team had broken a total of 23 world records prior to the 1956 Olympic Games in Melbourne, Australia. However, all hopes of prevailing at those Games were disrupted by the Hungarian revolution and Soviet invasion. Of all his teammates, Laszlo survived the Games the best with a fourth-place finish in the 1500 and sixth in the 5000.

27

Along with Coach Igloi, Laszlo and some of his Hungarian Olympic teammates defected to the United States directly from Melbourne. He resumed a successful running career for a number of years in the U.S. but was a man without a country in 1960, and he never competed in the Olympics again.

I knew little of the time between Laszlo's departure from running and how he came to coach at Valley College. But I did know that Mihaly Igloi coached at the University of Southern California campus and that the team competed under the name Los Angeles Track Club. The newly formed club at the time included Jim Beatty, Max Truex, Jim Grelle, Ron Larrieu, Joe Douglas, Bob Seaman and, for a brief time, Bob Schul. At one point there were five sub-four-minute milers on the team at once.

Upon Igloi's departure from the U.S., Joe Douglas took the reins as the coach. The team name changed when it moved to Santa Monica, where Joe continues to coach the Santa Monica Track Club. My late husband Tom Sturak ran under Joe for years, many of which paralleled my running time under Laszlo in the San Fernando Valley. Joe and Laszlo had both run for Igloi and coached similarly in a parallel existence.

When I first joined Judy Graham and Laszlo, we were members of a different Los Angeles Track Club. This was now an all-women and all-events club with distinguished coaches for the variety of specialties. Our star was the great Chi Cheng from Taiwan. At one of my first LATC meetings we viewed a movie of her recent European tour where she garnered many titles, records and glamorous awards. I was enthralled. A few years later the LATC disbanded. Laszlo and his ever-expanding group of followers eventually formed our own club: the San Fernando Valley Track Club.

While competing for the LATC, I ran my first track and field national championships in July 1971, competing in the 880. I had qualified winning my division in a regional meet, but losing the race to Becky Dennis. I had no idea what "AAU" was when told that I qualified for Amateur Athletic Union national championships. Laszlo said, "Of course you'll go."

Judy and I drove to Bakersfield for the meet, but my old VW bug couldn't make a tough climb over the mountains called the Grapevine. We were stranded until picked up by none other than the coach from another local women's club, Roy Swett, whose top runner was Debbie Heald. She was one of the best milers in our region, and in the nation. She later became a teammate of ours, but this was our first meeting.

In November that year I competed in my first cross-country national championships with the LATC. Running in snow in Cleveland, Ohio, I fell and broke my wrist, but I finished the race and was casted upon returning home.

Even at 2.5 miles, this was close to the longest distance I had ever raced. While still recovering from the wrist injury, I would be introduced to an event 10 times longer.

Laszlo Tabori with San Fernando Valley Track Club
runners (from left) Miki Gorman, Heather Tolford,
Leal-Ann Reinhart and me.

5. Marathon Start

Two roads diverged in a wood, and I
I took the one less traveled by,
And that has made all the difference.
Robert Frost

The last running event I witnessed in December 1971, the Western Hemisphere Marathon in Culver City, was momentous – both at the time and for what it would mean to me later. Laszlo Tabori actually lived right on the Culver City course, so he was always present for the race. My training partner Judy Graham and I joined him there that day because we had a teammate, Cheryl Bridges, who was running the marathon. She did not train with us but competed for the club.

We supported Cheryl in her marathon as she set a world record of 2:49:40, becoming the first woman to run under 2:50. I was intrigued. Watching Cheryl click off those miles over the marathon course looked like fun to me. She was strong but relaxed, a beautiful runner with great running form and a stride that just flowed.

The monument at the finish line of the Western Hemisphere Marathon lists the 1971 winner as "Patricia Bridges." Her first name changed only once, while her last name changed with every marriage: from Pedlow to Bridges to Flanagan to the current Treworgy. Her daughter is the Olympian Shalane Flanagan. (At the time we married, my husband made a good case for

31

women not to change last names, pointing out how it confuses track statisticians. I didn't change mine, nor did Shalane.)

Cheryl was an inspiration to me. I could not help but think that I could do what she did. I could run with her on the track and in cross-country, and perhaps I could do a marathon like her too. I vowed right then and there that I would try the Culver City race the next year.

However, returning to the track with Laszlo the following week, I was caught up in our routine schedule of indoor track in the winter, outdoor track in the spring and cross-country in the fall, with a little vacation time during summer before laying our base for the fall season. It was in that brief summer vacation that I was lured away from my usual loops around a park to venture out on the roads for a workout.

When I wasn't running on the track, my easy days were for running at Balboa Park in the San Fernando Valley. Judy and I were under strict orders to run only on dirt or grass surfaces, and I mean *always*. One day we met at Balboa at the same time a group of male runners were meeting for a road workout. Some of them also trained with us at the track, so we chatted.

They were led by a male runner in his 60s, Monty Montgomery. I'd seen this group regularly, and noted that they seemed to have a lot of fun, as they told stories and ran off on the roads headed for the beach and other interesting loops, while Judy and I ran in circles around the park. Twice I went with them, for a 10-miler and a 14-miler.

So when cross-country season ended in November with my best performance to date, eighth place in nationals, my thoughts turned back to that Western Hemisphere Marathon I wanted to do in December. I really wasn't prepared with any long runs in my repertoire except those two workouts I snuck in many months earlier.

I didn't let that stop me, and I asked Laszlo if I could enter (asking permission was requisite). I half-expected to be yelled at. After all, his attitude was that the marathon was something you ran if you were too slow to compete at the middle distances. However, what I received was almost philosophical. He said that there are some things I had to find out for myself, and that there were things he didn't try and would never know.

Besides, he added, I was the most stubborn runner he knew, and he thought I would go far. I still do not know if he meant "far" as in I had a future in marathoning, or "far" as in I'd go about 18 miles and drop out. No matter. I had his blessing, and that's what mattered.

I credited a college teammate, Mike Maggart, with getting me through the first 15 miles at seven-minute pace, and Doug Schwab for parking his bike and running the last mile in with me. (I ought to have been disqualified, I suspect.) In reality, I don't think my friends could ride their bikes near the end because my pace had slowed so much. As I wrote in my journal:

Those last four miles are almost unbearable, particularly the last two. Up to 22, it seemed almost a relaxed seven-minute pace. Then the race began for four miles. And worth every sore muscle – a thousand times over.

Cheryl Bridges did not run in the Culver City race that year, and I won my first marathon in a slow 3:15. I probably could have walked my final miles faster than I was running.

33

I recall that upon crossing that finish line I uttered the words "never again!" Later at the awards ceremony, however, I received my medal and thought how I would prepare differently for next time. I was hooked.

Interestingly enough, this race was a turning point for my family, who up to that point did not deem running to be worth my time. In fact, I fibbed about going out for a run with Judy that morning to cover up running in the marathon. I left a note on the table at home early that morning to say we went for a run, and made up some other excuse about shopping or a movie to buy more time for the day.

The only reason I had to make excuses was because it was the day for a family reunion at our house to celebrate Thanksgiving, my birthday and birthdays for several other relatives. I knew I'd be late, thus needing the excuse.

By winning the race, I was delayed by the awards ceremony and thought I would be in big trouble. However, when I snuck in the door and tried to slip into my seat at the dinner table, my family broke into applause. My aunt resided near the site of the marathon and had reported the whole thing, and then my winning photo had appeared on the local TV news.

With Cheryl (Bridges) Treworgy at the Western Hemisphere Marathon start/finish line monument in Culver City, California.

6. Boston 1973

Do not go where the path may lead,
Go instead where there is no path and leave a trail.
Ralph Waldo Emerson

Since my first marathon was also my first road race of any distance, I was not yet a seasoned enough road racer to know about the Boston Marathon. One of my training partners was marathoner Patrick Miller, who was originally from my hometown of Granada Hills and ran with Laszlo Tabori when he wasn't studying at Yale. After my win in Culver City, Patrick informed me that Boston would be an ideal goal now that the race officially had added a women's division. We discussed this with Laszlo, who agreed this would be the new goal for our training. This time we took the preparation seriously.

Laszlo had never been a road racer. One of the world's best at 1500 to 5000 meters in his era, he naturally trained me as a middle-distance runner. I had only modest success there, yet quite honestly the 1500-meter and mile races remained my favorite.

When I suggested running my first marathon, Laszlo told me, "The marathon is something you do when you're too slow to race anything shorter." Yet, as noted in Chapter 5, he didn't discourage me from running this distance.

My first attempt wasn't pretty, largely because I hadn't run far enough, often enough in training. The difference between my first two marathons is that I at least trained for Boston. Laszlo piled on the miles in intervals every other night during the week, and I piled on the miles on the roads on the weekends.

I arrived in Boston well trained – and feeling terribly homesick. But waiting for me there to cheer me up were beautiful gift baskets from home, filled with food and flowers. I recall first going to the highest viewpoint I could find, the top of the "Pru" (Prudential Center, the marathon finish line at the time). From 50 floors up. I could see all over town, spotting the obvious places to go for a run.

The most logical runner's route went along the Charles River. Once there, I made friends with runners along the way. I visited museums, the public library, old churches and parks. I tagged along with a team from Florida to watch a track meet one afternoon, and to the aquarium another time with local runners. On race day, we all piled onto school buses for the long ride out to the starting point in Hopkinton. I had to obtain a permission note from race director Will Cloney to ride the bus.

April in Boston could bring any kind of weather, and for me this usually has meant extreme weather. In this, my first trip, it was a heat wave, so starting at the then-traditional noon hour was not a welcome thought. I believe the men were herded into a gym, while the women runners were sheltered in a local chapel. It was a charming choice, if overly protective, now that I reflect on it.

There weren't many of us, as it was only the second year with an official women's division. I met the previous year's winner, Nina Kuscsik, who in time became one of my dearest friends and colleagues advocating for women's rights in running. I was also fortunate to meet previous unofficial winner Sara Mae Berman, but not until years later did I meet the first woman to finish Boston, Bobbi Gibb.

As I've indicated, I was not an experienced road runner, and my race-day preparation in outfitting myself at Boston is telling. I was thinking more like a hiker than a runner. To protect my feet, I wore two pairs of socks, one thin and snug, and a second layer of thick wool socks for cushioning. And, believe it or not, I chose to wear my heaviest training shoes with good, thick soles.

My shirt and shorts were chosen for looks. I knew the race was run on Patriot's Day, so I looked through my closet for something patriotic. I ended up with a white T-shirt embroidered with red and blue stars and stripes, and matched it with some blue-checkered shorts made out of terrycloth. (The shirt now resides in the BAA museum in Boston.)

The choice of shorts came back to haunt me, as well-intentioned sideline spectators showered us from garden hoses. Those shorts soaked up water like a towel, dragged to my knees and poured water down into my wool socks. I squeezed out the hems of my shorts, and my feet made squishing noises as I ran up Heartbreak Hill carrying extra water weight. I learned my lesson the hard way.

Tom Derderian wrote the book, *Boston Marathon*, for the centennial race edition, and his chapter on 1973 accurately depicts my experience. Tom wrote, "She had extraordinary talent, the speed that Berman, Kuscsik, Switzer and Gibb could only dream of... At last a very fast woman came to race at Boston, but unfortunately talent is not everything. Just as will-power alone cannot create the ability to run fast, neither can athletic talent without preparation, proper coaching and experience.

Jacqueline Hansen had a coach and had done preparation, but both were lacking. However, at the time she did not know it."

I don't remember a lot of the race, the course or the splits. But that's not unusual for me. I believe my gift is the ability to focus, in the process shutting out all outside distractions to the point I cannot recall the course after the race is over. I don't remember suffering any, but I suppose it's because I was a heat-trained California girl. I do know that I was afraid to eat or drink anything en route because my coach never allowed it on the track. (What did we know about distance running?)

The venerable Bud Collins wrote in the *Boston Globe* that I "seemed like Florence Nightingale entering a battalion aid station just behind the lines... The accompanying troops were bloody and bleary. Some were making it only in stretchers or wheelchairs... But there she was, upright and in command, La Hansen, waving shyly yet gratefully."

All the reporters latched onto my answer to their question about what I was going to treat myself to eat, although why is beyond me. I said the first thing that came into my head: "Going off training for a pizza and a root beer freeze" (from the Collins article). I received a dozen articles from all over the country quoting that line.

If only you knew when your 15 minutes of fame was at hand, you'd hope to say something more clever.

Winning the 1973 Boston Marathon.

7. "I Am a Runner"

Go confidently in the direction of your dreams.
Live the life that you have imagined.
H. D. Thoreau

Now that I'd won my first two marathons, Western Hemisphere in December 1972 and Boston in April 1973, my running career took a new turn and forever changed my life. I had found my event (and would go on to win 12 of my first 15 marathons).

It was with complete surprise and delight that I received my first invitation to a major road race when Don Cohen asked me to run in his Charleston (West Virginia) Distance Run, a 15-mile race in September 1973. I shared the good news with Laszlo Tabori, assuring him that while I had plans to go on a backpacking adventure with friends out of Vancouver for several weeks in July and August, I would be back in time for race day. Besides, I added, I'd take my running shoes, and whenever we made day camp I'd go off for long runs. The altitude would be an added benefit.

My optimism was met with less than enthusiasm. I remember the exchange like it was yesterday. Laszlo said that I would not be going hiking, that I would stay home and train. After all, he said, "you can hike when you're 84, but no one is going to pay to watch you run then."

My friends and I had made elaborate plans for the backpacking trip, so with great reluctance I complied with Laszlo's orders and called my traveling partners Gary Stormo and Jeff Rohr to break my disappointing news to them. Come to think of it, that actually was the day my running career changed; indeed my entire life changed. Previously the running supported backpacking and hiking, and now the hiking was disappearing from my life.

Flash forward many years to about 2009. I called Laszlo from a mountaintop in California to remind him of our long-ago conversation. I told him that even before 84 years of age, I realized he was right – that hiking was still an option and there wasn't a soul on earth who would now pay to watch me run.

Reflecting on my spring 1973 season after Boston, I competed in a collegiate meet on April 28, winning the mile (5:03) and half-mile (2:20.8) at San Diego State University. Both performances were school records and meet records. On April 29, I competed in the Mt. SAC Relays, winning the two-mile in 10:45 and qualifying (with the LATC) for AAU Nationals.

At the UCLA Collegiate Invitational on May 4, I won the mile (for CSUN) in 4:58, and wrote the press release for the school newspaper that began with "as the season closes, four girls advance from CSUN to the AIAW Nationals at Cal State-Hayward..." Becky Dennis and I trained with Laszlo, and we were the ones who were setting school and meet records. Since we had recruited these two other women, we even ran relays! On May 12, I won the AIAW mile title in 4:54, after running 5:04 in the trials the day before.

In late May, I won two other two-mile events: May 28 at Balboa Stadium in San Diego, I won the two-mile in 10:42. (In second place was 14-year-old Mary

Decker.) On June 10, at the State AAU Meet, I won the two-mile in 10:38 and our club won the team title.

When I wasn't training with Laszlo, I was running with the Cal State-Northridge (CSUN) track guys, some of whom trained with Laszlo at nearby L.A. Valley College. The spring season included a trip, organized by teammate Jon Sutherland, to run Bay to Breakers in San Francisco. I was second woman to my former teammate Cheryl Bridges. We also competed in a one-hour run in Santa Barbara, where I ran 9 miles, 1246 yards. (Later I became obsessed with that event and went over 10 miles twice in the following year.)

That summer at Pierce College we ran All-Comers meets, which were something to behold. These were standing-room-only events with all track and field events plus cross-country races. It was an accomplishment to qualify for the culminating meet at the end of the summer. My summer also included a Fourth of July 15K run in Santa Barbara, winning in 61:15, and a 5000-meter run three days later in 17:26, which I also won.

After my Boston victory I was doing press and media interviews frequently. Live TV shows really made me nervous, and I see from journal entries that I never went to these without dragging friends along in moral support, plus I was known to cancel a few appearances. I could've been on Johnny Carson and "Hollywood Stars," but I refused since I could not embarrass myself that way.

The big news that summer was that Laszlo switched our women's team from the L.A. Track Club to the Southern California Striders. (This was how I met my future husband, Tom Sturak, at the first team meeting.) The move included the male athletes from Laszlo's team, but I'm not sure how much they represented the club, as many of them were still running for their colleges.

Just days before my departure to Charleston, West Virginia, my new uniform arrived for the big event. Earlier that season, at Mt. SAC, John Bragg, the promotions representative for adidas, gave me new shoes and running gear, so I was all set for the trip. In those days adidas was the only company supporting women's track and field, generously giving running gear to any woman who qualified for national-level competition.

What a great sendoff it was when my friend Patrick Miller took me to see the 1972 Olympics documentary, "Visions of Eight." I wrote in my running journal, "So memorable!" I noted that arriving in Charleston I worked out early in the morning the day before the race "to beat the heat," and that I "sweat it out running along the river, but it was so pretty!" The lush green landscape, with the stifling humidity and deafening chirping insects and frogs, was a far cry from Southern California.

The pre-race day was filled with a press conference, luncheon, track clinic and a "fabulous dinner at the Cohens'." Guests included Steve Prefontaine, Jesse Owens and Dave Wottle, in addition to invited runners Neil Cusack, Tom Fleming, Jeff Galloway and Francie Larrieu.

Race day was described as "very hot, but clear," and "what a course, with the hill early in the race, at 2½ miles." I noted my time as 1:34 for first woman, 62nd overall. Francie Larrieu was second woman and 84th overall, and the men's race went to "Jeff Galloway, followed by [Lucien] Rosa, Cusack, [Jon] Anderson and Fleming, in that order."

A family friend, Greg Sorscek, came out to watch me run, so I even had my very own fan club of one. We celebrated at a big dinner party late that evening, and the next day I departed for home. I remarked in my journal how sore I was from the hilly course and had only managed a three-mile post-race run. On the other hand, I was richer for the store of memories that have stayed in my heart all these years.

The next journal entry noted the start of my senior year at CSUN the week I returned from Charleston. All my units were tied into a new cross-curriculum course entitled "Search for Identity." The course was taught by five professors who completely captivated me. My final portfolio about my own identity was entitled, what else, "I Am A Runner."

At the 1973 Charleston Distance Run, a 15-mile road race in Charleston, West Virginia.

8. Going International

Remember, they put their shorts on over their feet, just like you do.

Laszlo Tabori, on being afraid of the competition

In retrospect, the next two years after Boston could be called my peak in running. Of course, at the time it seemed like the improvements would never cease. All the runners I know think like that. One exception to the rule was the great miler, Filbert Bayi, who once said to me that running was like a flower blooming. One moment it's at the height of blossoming, and the next moment it's fading out and gone. Actually, he was speaking of making money in racing (since he was one of the many athletes my husband Tom Sturak represented as an agent).

During the 1974 track season, I won a six-mile race on the track in an American record time of 34:24. This gave me confidence for my first international trip, which in turn prepared me for closing out the year with another marathon on my "home course" in Culver City.

I was keenly aware by now that my new distance events did not afford me the opportunity to try out for the Olympic team, as was possible in the 800-meter or newly added 1500-meter races. I came to realize the injustice of having no place to advance to the highest level of the sport. Naively I imagined that a few letter-writing campaigns, circulating petitions and speaking out in the media would "get the job done." Little did I know that it would be a 10-year ordeal before seeing the marathon in the Olympics.

Dr. Ernst Van Aaken, hosted the first Women's International Marathon in Waldniel, West Germany. (Yes, there was still an East and West Germany.) I was not assigned to the official USA team because I had not participated in the U.S. National Marathon Championships. Those honors went to the winner and our first national marathon champion, Judy Ikenberry, and the next several women who placed behind her, providing they could afford to pay their own expenses to make the trip. They included Joan Ullyot, Lucy Bunz, Peggy Lyman and Ruth Anderson.

When Tom Sturak's best friend and training partner, Bruce Dern, heard this, he sponsored me to participate independently. However, once I was there the Germans treated me as part of the official U.S. delegation, including the team scoring.

Dr. Van Aaken was an early advocate of woman distance runners. He had been arguing the case for women since the 1950s, when he fought for a German national championships in 800 meters in 1954. A doubting journalist accused him of creating "Zatopeks in pigtails," recommending that ambulances and stretchers be on hand for the finish. That particular reporter later did an about-face, speaking of the "beauty and grace of the winner flying easily across the finish line."

It took Van Aaken another 15 years to implement the women's 1500 in the German federation's program. In 1973 he held his country's first women's marathon. He writes extensively about women, the "enduring sex," in his book *The Van Aaken Method* (a translation published by *Runner's World* in 1976, for which my husband wrote the introduction.) The book includes

48

pictures of Joan Ullyot and me with Dr. Van Aaken. Joan wrote about him in *Runner's World* magazine articles and in her 1976 book, *Women's Running.*

Here, from my running journal, is the report from my first European trip:

SEPTEMBER 19, Dusseldorf-Waldniel: Arriving in Dusseldorf was a moment of anticipation until we were met by a tall, lean young man identified by a handwritten "marathon" sign. I was recognized by the shoes and my size. As he said, short, small and quick.

Later I was to discover this was Van Aaken's nephew, Jochen, and he acted as a valuable translator, chauffeur, running mate and good friend.

To my delight, I had the pleasure of meeting the legendary Doctor at the first event of the day.

Through the translations by Joan Ullyot, we were able to converse – not only at the press conference, but en route to Holland this P.M. and later, in a casual gathering at his home.

The workout with Jochen revealed a very nice, flat course for Sunday's race. In the dark, Jochen was careful to point out every obstacle, shouting "Attention!"

It should be a very fast race – providing we don't all become fat as pigs from all the great food. Marie's homegrown, home-cooked dinners are the best ever!

SEPTEMBER 20, Waldniel: A good night's rest (under feather beds) made for a nice A.M. run around the course. Although Judy [Ikenberry] and some [others] sped about the loop, I stayed safely in the company of Tom, Joan and Ruth [Anderson] at a sensible pace. Oh, and Gerta Reinke too – she ran at Boston in 1973. "Sensible" meant only six or seven kilometers. And in the daylight I could see the beauty our course runs through.

After a breakfast of fresh rolls and homemade cherry jam with tea (most preferred coffee) and eggs boiled. These hearty appetites are strange to our hostess, Marie, but she tolerates them.

This afternoon we all shopped in downtown Dusseldorf. The square was so elegant and modern, but prettiest was the elm-lined canal in the center of the street... not to forget the gorgeous statue – Father Rhine – amid a rushing fountain.

One precious purchase I made on this spree was this leather-bound journal, which the good Doctor was kind enough to inscribe as we sat next to Father Rhine.

By the way, I was surprised when he suggested we stop for "sweets" after seeing the girls gawking at the bakery window. He even ate a big piece of chocolate cream pie! Tom and I had a wonderful ice cream delight covered with cherries (not the awful marinated kind). I have a souvenir spoon.

SEPTEMBER 21, Waldniel: I am convinced the Doctor is as zany as anyone. This morning he rode about the streets shouting things about the marathon over the P.A. system atop his Mercedes. Achtung! Achtung! Certainly, it's not the behavior I expected from the general staunch German way!

And Marie's eccentricities charm me. To drink cold milk is uncivilized, as is a sloppy room and bare feet – one might get "eczema." She certainly tolerates a lot from us, probably thanks entirely to Judy's charming manner. No one else has access to that immaculate kitchen, yet Judy managed pancakes tonight for the Americans.

At this evening's reception, guest competitors were introduced, speeches made, interviews and photos taken. Overall a pleasant gathering.

Feeling more relaxed at this point, because of the team's jovial attitude, I think it's probably for the best. The starting line will bring enough tension.

I happened to tell one reporter my one wish was to convey my desire to see the marathon for women in the Olympics. Very impressed, she wants that broadcasted tomorrow. Voila!

Note: Of all the speeches made tonight, I think that Joan wins the award for her charm and general acceptance by all. The joke in reference to the Doctor being a little bit crazy was well received and agreed. Bouquets literally to Dr. Joan!

To capture the feelings going through me the morning of this race is very difficult, but worth the attempt. I slept well. In fact, while others ate and Tom ran, I just slept until the last minute. I suppose others think my peculiarities are a "psych." I really don't know and do not care. I slept, didn't eat and didn't fret about pace times. So what? I simply relaxed as best I could mentally and tried to get in the "groove" of the race.

Some runners strike me as very superstitious. For instance, I've abandoned the club uniform for an old red shirt and shorts – more comfortable and familiar actually. Since our federation won't allow me to represent the USA, for foregoing the national marathon championships, I was not issued a U.S. uniform. The club uniform wouldn't be meaningful overseas, so I chose this plain, red uniform.

SEPTEMBER 22, Waldniel: I was ecstatic with my fifth-place overall finish, first American finisher and breaking three hours for my first time. Post-race, I reflected on how I might run faster next time. In the moment, I thought I ran sensibly, gently, losing nothing by taking no risks, and enjoyed the success. Although

51

the course was flat, with simple repeated 10-kilometer loops to follow, and the organization of the race was impeccable, yet the cold, hard winds throughout the entire race were not conducive to fast times. So I was proud of my much anticipated time improvement at 2:56:25.

Feeling lots of pride, I accepted my generous awards and gifts that evening: a gorgeous silver trophy cup, a beautiful bouquet of flowers, a certificate and medal as well as a second-place team certificate and medal. Every item was prepared with class, and presented graciously. Afterward the athletes exchanged autographs, T-shirts and patches, posters and pins. The celebration that followed was great fun.

At first International Women's Marathon in Waldniel, West Germany, with (right of me) Joan Ullyot, Lucy Bunz and Nina Kuscsik.

9. World Leader

Yeah, it's been a long time coming
Never thought it'd take so long
I stood still but time kept running
Time has made me strong
Time has been a long time waiting
Waiting for this day to come
And time don't wait so I keep singing
Yeah, it's been a long time coming
Never thought it'd take so long
I would, I stood still and time kept running
And time has made me strong
And made me strong
And made me strong
Time has made me strong
Jonny Lang

Going to Waldniel for the marathon was only the beginning of what became a grand tour through Germany, Italy, Tunisia and France over a 25-day period (carrying our Frommer's book, *Europe on $10 a Day*).

We left rainy, windy Waldniel the day after the women's marathon and traveled by train to Nurnburg, where adidas representatives were hosting me at the adidas Hotel in Herzogenaurach. The following morning, Tom and I took a run in the prettiest forests right behind our hotel. We were treated to a tour of the

53

shoe factory, and received gifts in shoes, bags and sweatsuits.

The mass production of hand-sewn shoes, rows of women stitching, was a sight I would never forget. Also I had the good fortune to meet company founder Adi Dassler himself and his wife, who was astonished at my running feats. She feigned a faint at the mention of running a marathon.

I recorded a lot of meals along with my miles during that journey. The food was usually impressive, if simple, always healthy, and of course delicious. Dinner with the Dasslers was done with exquisite perfection from the mushroom soup, filet of sole and salad to dessert with cherries over ice cream. Wine from the region was served with every course, or as Adi Dassler said, "wine with heart."

The next day I found the Dassler Trail in the woods, which had a name that meant "trim fit," "keep trim" or some such term. The trail ran by ponds with geese and, from the hills, overlooked small villages below. Our last day there was beautiful and sunny as our adidas-clad driver collected us in his Mercedes and we were off for the train station.

Our next stop was in Bavaria to meet Eugen Brutting, who manufactured shoes that later came to be called "Lydiards" in the United States, although this was just one model of Brutting shoes. Collecting more shoes, bags and sweats, I was beginning to question the wisdom of my choice to travel with my backpack.

From there we traveled to Munich to see the site of the last Olympic Games, staying in what had been part of the athletes' housing, in a "sport hotel." The one error in my German translation of the menu resulted in "calf's tongue" for dinner, the thought of which was the only repulsive moment of my trip, at least thus far.

From there we traveled through Germany and Italy, toward Tunisia where Tom and I stayed with friends. They were members of Tom's training group at home, the Santa Monica Track Club. The husband, Hiro Hadjeri, was Tunisian and he spent several months every year in Tunis. His wife Pam was working on an article for *Runner's World* on the Tunisian Olympian, Mohamed Gammoudi, whom I looked forward to meeting.

En route, while traveling through Italy, I won a 15K in Florence, breaking a women's world record in 52:15 as I finished seventh overall, trailing right behind Tom, who was very surprised. In fact, the times for fifth, sixth and seventh places were all identical.

I found the Italian race interesting because men showed they definitely did not want me to pass them. They would speed up to recapture the lead, only to fade away eventually. Afterward one man emerged from the crowd to tell me, "I have always said that the day I am beaten by a woman is the day I stop running, but today I have learned something." I still cherish that liberated man's comments!

While we waited for the awards ceremony, Tom and I were perusing the merchandise awards to be distributed. He suggested I choose something to eat, drink or wear, since we were trying to lighten our baggage and we still had to jog back to our hotel for departure by train right away. However, I received a bouquet of red carnations, a medal (thankful it wasn't another trophy), and the most cumbersome and I dare say sexist item deemed fitting for the woman winner – an iron; yes, an electric flat iron.

As we ran off, I gave away flowers one by one to children, the iron went to my hotel landlady, and the medals were tucked into our luggage despite the race director's concern they would get us in trouble at the U.S. border. The race was part of some political rally by the Socialist party, about which I had no knowledge. Of course the flowers were red, as were the banners and the stage decorations.

We had stayed overnight in Florence only because we were too exhausted from difficult travel on the standing-room-only trains. Otherwise we might never have discovered this race. We identified it from a poster (which I kept as a souvenir) hanging in a gelato shop the night before. Waking up in Florence was like visiting a museum. The vista of the tiled roof buildings was spectacular.

The Florentine hills were beautiful, but not so enticing when I discovered the 15K race course went over them. Oddly, we were given a three-part race number. I thought one might be pinned to my bag for retrieval, one on the front and one on the back of my shirt. But no, I was corrected by charades (no one spoke English, and I spoke no Italian) to wear all three on my front. Every five kilometers, a judge stepped out to stamp the sequence of numbers! I steered clear of the first checkpoint official because I thought I was being accosted, until I figured out his role. I guess that's a way of catching cheaters, but I wondered if the leaders slowed down for that.

Traveling to Venice, Rome and Naples were each day-trips only, doing all our sightseeing combined with running. From Naples we took a boat to Palermo and flew from there to Tunis.

When we met Mohamed Gammoudi in Tunis, I felt quite honored to join him in a training run on the military base where he and his teammates trained. I respectfully wore long pants, as running shorts on women were completely unacceptable in that country.

Our conversations took place in three languages, translated from Arabic to French to English and in reverse, so there was a lag time between questions and answers. I was asked how the pace was, and to give my answer in a percentage of effort. When I said it was easy, maybe 50 percent, I recognized the response in gasps before the translation. Those men did not expect a woman who could hold pace with them, I suppose.

It was an interesting time visiting our friend Hiro's family in Tunis during the holy month of Ramadan, when Muslims don't eat or drink between sunrise and sunset. (However, Tom and I were allowed to help ourselves in the kitchen during the day.) Meals continued to leave an indelible impression on me, although they were of course prepared for consumption only after sundown. By the end of each day of fasting, the meal was truly a feast of great magnitude.

Preparation was labor-intensive, right down to the bowls full of pomegranate seeds sprinkled with rose water for dessert. Sounds simple enough, but imagine pulling out all those thousands of seeds! I watched as servants worked all day in preparation. I brought home several new and enticing recipes, naturally all in French.

Upon returning home from my first European experience, I held newfound confidence that I could run with the "best of them." And I didn't mean the men from Tunis or even the men of Florence, but I meant the best women in Waldniel and throughout the world.

Back in Los Angeles I resumed training with Laszlo Tabori in mid-October, on a schedule designed for the December marathon in Culver City but including cross-country races. My mileage rose from 70 to 90 miles per week, then topped out at 110 miles before the marathon week.

This preparation included many races. Perhaps the most indicative of my marathon fitness was the Long Beach Prep 16.2-mile race. As the title indicates, this was a benchmark race for the Western Hemisphere Marathon. I ran 1:38:58 – a 6:06 mile pace.

I also ran the district cross-country championships in 18:41 for 3.5 miles and the AAU state meet in San Diego, 17:28 for 5000 meters in fourth place. My last race before the marathon, two weeks later, was a 10.09-mile, in which I broke six-minute pace.

As I had for the Waldniel marathon, I again put myself on the carbo-load diet, depleting carbohydrates the first part of the week and increasing protein consumption, followed by a transition day and then increasing carbohydrates in the latter part of the week leading up to the race. This was supposed to enable my body to maximize storage of carbohydrates as a source of energy to fuel the long race. I was pleased that this time I did not become nauseous like before.

On Western Hemisphere race day in December 1974, as I warmed up with our friend Bruce Dern, we talked about how others were projecting records for me and my nervous anticipation. He told me he loved his ability to pick winners (as the one who sponsored my trip to the international women's marathon in Germany when I did not "make" the USA team) and that I should not pay any attention to the pressure, just run my own pace, my own race. I calmly went to the starting line, calmly set my pace, calmly shut out the bystanders and crossed the finish line in a new world record of 2:43:55. Thank you, Bruce!

In retrospect, although I was really pleased with the time and especially the record, the race was not necessarily a life-changing event. I logged the finish time into my journal as "N.W.R. (new world record) at

Culver City marathon." We had a team party a week later, where my racing shoes were placed in the Helms Athletic Foundation museum in Culver City by founder Bill Schroeder, and the adidas rep, John Bragg, presented me with new ones.

My training resumed without pause. I went running the next day with Monty Montgomery and the guys around Balboa Park, then did a regular Laszlo workout the following night. I was already back into middle-distance training for the indoor season.

With Olympic 5000-meter champion (1968) Mohamed Gammoudi in Tunisia.

10. "Peak Performance"

We never know how high we are
Till we are called to rise
And then, if we are true to plan
Our statures touch the skies.
                                    Emily Dickinson

Naturally, as 1975 dawned, I couldn't predict it would be such a good year. Then I didn't realize as the year ended that it would stand as my best ever. Like most athletes in their heyday, I imagined that improvements in performance would never cease. We only see in retrospect when we hit our peak, and why.

One reason 1974-75 went so well was consistently solid training. Apart from an off-month in February 1974, due to illness and injury, I averaged 340 miles a month pretty consistently for a year's total of 3882 miles. Then in 1975 my mileage totaled 4142 miles and the months were more evenly paced (so to speak).

That year opened with indoor track, then outdoor track where I focused on the two-mile and 5000 meters. Included were a few longer road races: a half-marathon, a 10K, a 15K and in summer a 30K. I ran one of my favorite events, the one-hour run on the track in a quest to get beyond 10 miles, doing so twice (by 112 and 243 yards) in a week's span.

I think the key to success in 1975 was having all these stepping stones in progression. My training was consistently solid but not excessive, and races built toward the fall season and my first marathon of the year.

In June, I was traveling from San Juan, Puerto Rico, where I'd won a 30-kilometer road race. My flying partners were Bill Rodgers and Tom Fleming. Bill, the men's victor, had a rougher time of it than I did. We shared the same support crew, who promised to be at every 5K mark with our replacement drinks. This was crucial in the stifling heat and humidity. I doubted I'd ever see them because Bill would be so far ahead that they'd never wait for me.

At the first 5K mark, they showed up on their motorcycle with my water bottle – and then I never saw them again. When I started to fade, I at least had such a big lead that I could shut the engine down and coast in. Bill never saw this crew again either, but he had to battle to the finish to win – and landed in the hospital to recover.

At that race, we met a Brazilian man named Getulio who was extending invitations to his race in Sao Paulo, the Sao Silvestre midnight run on New Year's Eve. He was asking the elite field in general who would be interested in racing there. Naturally I said yes. He was quite embarrassed to inform me that it had always been a men-only race. Naturally, I asked why!

Getulio said he would go back to Brazil and talk with the race director and committee members to see about adding a women's event. I promised him I would help him to build that field. We would stay in communication.

Departing San Juan, Tom Fleming, Bill Rodgers and I flew back to the States where I was entered to run the 3000 meters in the U.S. track and field national championships four days later, in Tom's hometown in New Jersey. We arrived at the airport departure gate with a trophy more than half my height. It brought a lot of attention and questions, all positive except for the stewardess's. She only saw it as a dangerous projectile in the cabin of the plane. Thus, as my trophy sat buckled in a first-class seat, I was back in a fully occupied coach section, complete with screaming infants driving everyone crazy, their parents included.

I also noted in my journal that I was reading *Women Sports* magazine and chatting with so many people about the women distance runners' exclusion from the Olympics that I felt moved to the point of radical action. Inevitably the conversation would end up with the assumption that anyone who held a world record must be going to the Olympic Games – and why not? I concluded that it was a very good question.

My journal notes captured my thoughts and brainstorming, which included, "I wonder if anyone's asked the IOC?" and, "If not, I want to... but how?" And I laid out my case as I saw it. It even included, "After all alternatives are exhausted, how about a 'run-in' at Montreal [1976 Olympics]?"

Landing in New Jersey, I ran that 3000 in the national championships. But the 30K race in the heat and humidity of San Juan left my running self too exhausted for the short, fast-paced race. As if the long race and travel fatigue weren't enough, there was the matter of the shave-ice treat I ingested in San Juan, not thinking about the water source for that ice. In the New Jersey race, I placed eighth. Nonetheless, the trip was an unexpected stepping stone to advance opportunities for me – and ultimately a lot more women – to run another day.

In 1975, I passed up the women's national marathon championships once again, in part due to a scheduling conflict and in part because I did not believe my mileage and training were adequate for a marathon. Instead I focused on a little known but promising new race in Eugene, Oregon, the Nike-Oregon Track Club Marathon, in the fall season.

My mileage did not reach the 100-plus per week that I thought was necessary for marathon training. The result was so outstanding that I took this as a lesson and never ran over 100 miles a week again.

This marathon is one race of perhaps only two in my life that I would label a "peak performance." In both cases, racing was effortless and euphoric. To look back and apply sports psychology terminology, I would say that I took all the steps necessary to produce a classic peak performance. One of those steps was announcing my goal before the race. I understand now that "declaration" is part of the process, making the goal real by telling others.

I was on a tune-up run a few days before this race, getting a tour of Eugene on my first visit there. The town was mourning the death of Steve Prefontaine, from his accident just five months earlier. The running tour included places where Pre ran, where he raced, where he crashed.

Eventually the running conversation went, "So what sort of time are you aiming for?" Somehow it just rolled off my tongue. "Six-minute miles," I said. That must have sounded presumptuous! The comment was met with dead silence, followed by hushed murmurs while adding up the figures – which would result in a 2:37 marathon, a world record and the first sub-2:40.

On race day, it all came together. I chose Eugene, knowing that the course would be relatively flat, the day cool, maybe drizzly, and, most importantly, the course accurately measured. The Nike-OTC Marathon was run on what was to be the men's Olympic

Marathon Trials course the next year – a dress rehearsal, as it were. The race met all those expectations.

Plus, I came into the race feeling good about my workouts. Even my coach, Laszlo Tabori, said at the close of that last interval workout the week before I departed, "You're ready." That comment came after the two five-minute mile repeats I did in the middle of the workout. Even though I questioned the connection, I trusted Laszlo to know these things.

Joe Henderson printed that workout, along with several others from my last big pre-marathon week, in his book *Road Racers and Their Training*:

TUESDAY: 2½-mile warm-up; 15 x 100 shakeups (eight medium, seven hard); 10 x 400 with three hard (73, 71, 72 seconds); 2½ laps easy; eight x 150 (two medium, one hard); five laps hard (5:13 mile); two laps easy; five laps hard (5:17 mile); 2½ laps easy; 10 x 200 (two hard, two medium); two laps easy; 12 x 100 shakedowns (two medium, one hard).

MONDAY AND WEDNESDAY: My favorite workout of "25-lappers" both mornings, and an eight-mile run one evening and a nine-mile run the other.

THURSDAY: A modified interval workout, easier than Tuesday's because I had a race on Saturday.

FRIDAY: A brief pre-race run.

SATURDAY: A 16:55 cross-country 5K race.

SUNDAY: My last long run of 19 miles before departing for Eugene the next week.

Those 25-lap workouts were the best! You could do them anywhere, anytime, without using a stopwatch. I ran a continuous 25 laps consisting of a five-lap warm-up, then repeated sets of four laps per set: 2 x 100 medium, 2 x 150 build-up, 2 x 100 medium and 2 x 100 hard with an easy jog on the curves in between each.

This is what the sets looked like: (lap one) run 100 meters medium hard on each straight of the track, while jogging the curves; (lap two) build-up speed for 150 meters, starting at the middle of the curve, running down the whole straight, jogging only the rest of the curve; do this twice, for each side of the track; (lap three) repeat the same lap one; (lap four) repeat the same pattern for lap one, but run the straights hard. These four laps constitute one set, and if repeated five times, equals 20 laps.

My friends in Eugene, Janet and Tom Heinonen, arranged for my housing with the Ledbetter family. Young Lili Ledbetter was a local high school track star. We became good friends, and her mom made the best-ever zucchini bread complete with homegrown filbert nuts. I jokingly say that my race was fueled on zucchini bread; I enjoyed it so much.

Throughout the race, Janet and Lili could be found bicycling from station to station, either making sure my bottles of Gookinaid were waiting for me, or more so to check on my progress and splits. I once said in a *Sports Illustrated* article that "there were days I could run forever." Gratefully this was one of those days.

To say it felt effortless sounds overly boastful, but it was true. In review, my splits averaged 6:02 per mile, none was slower than 6:10, and my last five miles were at 5:55. I usually could not do the math when running tired. But that day when I heard my 20-mile split, the math told me I was ahead of world-record pace. So I immediately took off, leaving behind the group of male runners that had accompanied me to that point. Looking back, a move like that with six miles to go could have ended badly, but that day it worked.

I regained the world record I'd lost earlier that year (to Liane Winter of West Germany, who ran 2:42:24;

her countrywoman Christa Vahlensieck bettered that mark soon afterward, with 2:40:16). I also earned the everlasting title of being the first woman to break 2:40 by running 2:38:19.

World record finish at Nike-OTC Marathon, Eugene, Oregon, in 1975.

11. Hawaii to Brazil

Progress lies not in enhancing what is, but in advancing toward what will be.
Kahlil Gibran

I can't recall where the credit goes, but someone once wrote about my ability to string together successful back-to-back performances – such as Waldniel-Florence-Culver City in late 1974. After all the training and focus that went into my Nike-OTC in October 1975, traveling to Hawaii and then Brazil that December was a pleasure. But I also felt I owed my hosts, and myself, good efforts. I won one of these races and finished a close second in the other, so while these were enjoyable trips abroad, they were not purely vacations.

HONOLULU MARATHON

Leal-Ann Reinhart and I flew to Honolulu on December 11, 1975, for the marathon and were met by Virginia Moore, who offered to host us in her home in the Kailua bay area. I noted in my journal that we went for an eight-mile run and it was beautiful in every sense, the scents and sights. That evening we enjoyed a gathering of other runners, and arose the next morning for another beautiful eight-mile run. The temperatures were mild, the sky was slightly overcast, and it rained off and on all day, but was enjoyable. That afternoon

67

we attended a press conference at the race headquarters, the Sheraton Waikiki, where we met the Chun family (known as the "Hunky Bunch") and Jack Scaff. There was a pre-marathon carbo-load dinner that evening for everyone. The weather continued with off-and-on rain through the night and the following day, and we ran just four miles.

The race (on December 14) began before the sun rose, at Aloha Tower in Honolulu. Virginia and I left the house around 4:30 A.M. to park the car at the finish line and bus over to the start. It was dark en route and often drizzly, but never cool. The ride from Kailua was uneventful and neither of us spoke much, both a little nervous.

Leal-Ann and Virginia's spouse Tom were planning to see us about five miles into the race, so they were home either sleeping or eating breakfast when we left. I was hoping all would go well and that our elaborate plans for dispensing my ERG (Gookinaid) every three miles would work out. Under such hot and humid conditions, this would be a vital factor in the race.

By the time we reached Kapiolani Park, I knew the humidity would be high. As it turned out, 85 percent was the official report. The bus picked up more runners at the Princess K. Hotel. Earl and Barbara Rippee and Laszlo Tabori boarded there. Was he ever decked out for the race – in green shorts, an SFVTC T-shirt and green and white running shoes. It was the first time he had ever accompanied me for a road race, and I guess he was prepared to do it all on foot if need be.

It was still dark when we arrived at Aloha Tower, but I soon discovered that the heat was already intense. It didn't take a second thought to decide to run shirtless. So after a brief warm-up, I left my shirt with Barbara and headed to the starting line, 705 others with me.

There was nothing remarkable about the start. Nothing except perhaps being placed on the line with Kenny Moore, Steve Hoag and Jeff Galloway. Needless to say, I held my own pace and stayed back until the rush went by. It was sort of eerie running along in the dark for the first three miles or so. Not only were the streets vacant of spectators and automobiles, but also I saw no sign of the runners before me at times and no sign of assisting officials. As I ran through numerous red stoplights, I just hoped I was still on course.

Before long, the five-mile mark came up at 31 minutes. A little slow but more believable than the 6:00 mile and 11:43 two-mile times I heard earlier. The next five miles were also in 31 minutes, and so were the next five miles. Even, but slow.

I drank all the ERG I could get down every three miles when Leal-Ann and Tom zipped by on their motorbike to make a pit stop for me. But nothing was feeling good, and I couldn't overcome the awful nausea I kept experiencing. Somehow I kept remembering running in San Juan. Again this was definitely the humidity and its ill effects.

Other than the misery, I guess I most remember Laszlo running various segments of the race, including the final hill. Goodness knows I needed some encouragement. (But I doubt he needed the workout he got.) All in all, it was an okay performance, I resolved. I didn't run my best time, but then again that would have meant another world record. The conditions were simply not conducive to a world-record time and I felt lucky to win. It was certainly nice to cross the finish tape, receive a seed necklace and a beautiful lei of double carnations. Smothered with the good scents of the flowers and caught up in interviews and photographs, I had little time for remorse about running

69

2:49. I was indeed content to have finished in relatively good condition.

Before too long, I was greeting Cindy Dalrymple, second-place finisher in 2:54, and Joan Ullyot, who finished third in 3:02. Eileen Waters was fourth and also ran a good time of 3:12. Hard to believe, I learned later, that a total of 95 women completed this marathon. That was more than in any of my marathons to date.

The awards ceremony was really neat. Everyone attended in picnic style with plenty of food to share. Trophies and plaques were exquisite, and victors of numerous divisions were recognized. The awards were beautifully designed blocks of wood with lava rocks mounted on them and a plaque engraved with the event, division and donor's name. First-place trophies were distinguished by a metal sculpture of the "King's Runner" (appropriate as the rocks came from the King's Highway). After the blessing of the rocks, the presentation ceremony took place and speeches were made on behalf of those responsible.

Tom and Doris Ferguson directed this whole production, adequately covering every possible detail. Accordingly they were awarded their own trophy, engraved "First in the hearts of 700 runners." Nothing could have been more appropriately put, and the standing ovation vouched for that fact. Other happy recipients were the Chuns winning the family division as well as individual awards. Daven ran a PR of 2:52 and May took first in her division, presenting her trophy to her sister June, who through a mishap was unable to finish the race. This typified the genuine goodwill spirit about this family and all the people I met in Hawaii.

I had the good fortune to meet the Hunky Bunch on this, my first, trip to Hawaii. Similar to television's "Brady Bunch," mom and dad were each previously divorced, each with three children, all teenagers. Mom, Connie, had three daughters and Dad, nicknamed Hunky, had three sons. As *Sports Illustrated* wrote about them in 1974, they "may not have been the country's first family, but they were probably the fastest."

Staying at their home was impressive. At the doorstep, shoes were stored – so many it took a floor to ceiling set of shelves divided into cubes to hold all the running shoes this family of eight – with each one's initials written on the heels of each shoe to keep them organized. In the yard, numerous chickens and rabbits were housed, plus at least three dogs and a pig by the name of Suey.

Household chores were posted on a chalkboard, listed in sister-brother pairings. Medals, ribbons and trophies were strewn all over the interior of the house. The Christmas tree stayed up until at least Valentine's Day. At any given time of the day, some stage of meal preparation seemed to be taking place. Everyone participated in preparing meals, and I learned new recipes for stir-fried Chinese meals. By the time I went home, I acquired a new chopping block, wok and utensils.

On Monday after the race, Leal-Ann and I went sightseeing around Oahu, delaying our plan to go to Maui for one more day. We regretfully made the mistake of not checking the bus schedule, and we spent most of the day waiting on buses and going in the wrong direction at times. At any rate, we saw a whole lot of the island and finished with a workout at Kapiolani Park with two loops of about 2½ miles each. After saying farewells to Earl and Barbara, Laszlo and Kati, we rushed back to Kailua and treated Virginia and Tom to their favorite Mexican restaurant.

On Tuesday we got to the airport in time to fly to Maui earlier than planned. The flight was only 20 minutes, and thus we had a good early start on our day. At the Maui airport we rented a car to drive to Hana. Johnny Faerber had arranged housing with a friend there. First we stopped at Baldwin Park, located a short distance from the airport on the road to Hana. It's a great place to camp, picnic and swim, but we ran. Our loop encompassed not only the baseball field but the golf course as well, and nobody seemed to mind.

I really enjoyed our drive to Hana. Leaving the fields of sugar cane, we started switch-backing up the mountains through lush fern grottos, waterfalls and tropical forests. It was like falling into paradise to arrive in Hana 53 miles later. But the paradise wouldn't be so if it were any easier to get there. I sincerely hope the town can stay small.

In this town of 750 or so, we inquired about a phone to call the Getzens and were informed that Bob was still working and Syd was still at school. We were at the renowned Hasagawa Store. The only two public phones were being repaired, but as we talked with the repairman, a VW van drove up. "Are you going to stay with us?" asked the driver asked, who turned out to be Bob.

Settled into our new abode, Bob led a running tour of Hana. When we ran up to the cliffs of the local bay, I was reminded of running with Bill Gookin in San Diego on Sunset Cliffs. As it turned out, Bill is a mutual friend Bob and I have in common. We investigated the caves and beaches and then ran up to the highest point in town for a gorgeous panoramic view. A memorial is placed there for Tom Fagan, who founded Hana Ranch.

After dinner, we chatted and planned the tour of Maui. From the time we left our temporary home in Oahu, Leal and I both felt we were beginning a whole exciting new adventure. Indeed we were! The highlight was hiking at Haleakala and camping overnight (and nearly freezing). We cherished the sunrise on the crater.

The next and final day in Maui, we took a four-mile run, left for the airport and arrived in Honolulu by 9:30 A.M. First we went to the Fergusons' and then to the Chuns' for a five- to six-mile run, dinner, and helped put together the finishers' results for distribution. We spent the next two days with the Chuns, including a Tantalus run, shopping for souvenirs to take home, a visit to Chinatown and plenty of great meals. We returned to Los Angeles on December 21. It was an excellent adventure, one long remembered.

SAO SILVESTRE

I mentioned in Chapter 10 that my experience in Puerto Rico provided an unexpected step forward for women runners. Long story short, Brazilian race official Getulio and I kept in touch as promised, and he succeeded in convincing the race committee for the Sao Silvestre New Year's Eve race in Sao Paulo to open a women's division. I helped him build the field with the best women runners in the world. I included Christa Vahlensieck of West Germany (outdoing myself), who was the inaugural female winner while I took second.

While in Brazil, I reunited with some of my European running acquaintances, including Christa and her coach Manfred Steffny, and Noel Tamini of *Spiridon* magazine. Some of those I met in Puerto Rico were participating in Sao Paulo as well. I also had the pleasure of meeting the South African runner, Titus

Mamabola, who spoke of Goodenough and the Colonel (whom I'd met in Puerto Rico).

Perhaps the most anticipated meeting was with Emil Zatopek, a kind person, master of multiple languages and obviously well admired the world over, particularly here in Sao Paulo as the welcoming lines of people were evident. I was thrilled when Emil gave me his *Spiridon* jacket one day on a walk. Gaston Roelants, Belgium steeplechaser and cross-country runner, joined us and I enjoyed his company.

Most of my pre-race workouts were done with Garry Bjorklund and some of the Australians and Italians. Getulio sometimes drove us to places to train, but mostly we ran the streets from the hotel. Not wanting to be left behind, I always ran too fast, and we were dodging cars all the time. It was not worth running on the streets. But the worst mistake was running my track workout, a bunch of 220s, delayed too late in the week plus running them on a cinder track. My calf muscles were so sore that I could barely run after that. It was a disaster for my race. Plus, the humidity and heat during the race made me recall San Juan all over again.

This trip brought me back home the first week of January 1976. I looked forward to another successful year, but it wouldn't go as smoothly as the previous two had gone.

Winning the Honolulu Marathon in 1975.

12. Seventy-Sicks

You gain strength, courage and confidence by every experience in which you really stop to look fear in the face. "I lived through this horror. I can take the next thing that comes along." You must do the thing you think you cannot do.

Eleanor Roosevelt

The world record was a hard act to follow in 1976. That year did not produce any significant personal records, and it seemed like every other week I was seeing a doctor. So many races were described with variations on the word *sick*.

There were some fun runs like the Daisy Hill 13.5-mile run in January, with Joan Ullyot. We ran under assumed names, because neither of us were feeling well and Joan did not want to have a bad race ruin her grand-prix points. I went along and ran as "Susan B. Anthony." Imagine my surprise when "Sue" was called to the stage to receive her award for (inadvertently) winning the race.

The Southern California District Championship race for 30 kilometers was held in Culver City in February. Again I was not feeling well and almost didn't run at all.

Tom Sturak's usual response to my complaints such as this was to tell me an Abebe Bikila story. He was so tough, he could have his appendix out one day and win the Olympic gold medal the next, and run barefoot at that. Tom exaggerated (Bikila won his second Olympic marathon weeks after his appendectomy – and wearing shoes), but I saw his point that I should not complain so much.

Well, that day I started slowly, but feeling better each lap of the three-lap course, I sped up each round and ended up winning in an age-group record. Tom developed an I-told-you-so attitude about those Bikila stories.

March produced a fair race at the 25K in Lunada Bay for a time of 1:35:39. Then in April, I really enjoyed sharing a 14-mile two-person relay with Leal-Ann Reinhart, finishing in 78:25.

After the race, Leal-Ann and I went to Dr. Barbara Drinkwater's lab at UC Santa Barbara to run on her treadmill for one of her research studies. We were often guinea pigs for Dr. Drinkwater's studies.

This particular test was to measure the effects of heat on running performance, and it involved treadmills in various rooms with increasing temperatures up to 118 degrees. Leal had a more efficient cooling system than I. The lab technicians pulled me off at some point when my core temperature started to soar and I wasn't sweating.

Even though I won the Avenue of the Giants Marathon in May, it was one of my worst performances as I felt sick the entire route. I made some bad judgment calls. The more dehydrated I became, the more nausea and cramps set in, and the more I was inclined not to drink, exacerbating the problem.

Perhaps that marathon was ill advised in the first place, since the following weekend I was entered in the New York Mini-Marathon for women. In fact, I flew directly from San Francisco after the marathon, which was an awful trip. I wasn't physically able to run right up to the New York 10K race, where I placed second in 36:03. I have to wonder what I was thinking, making such a plan.

Later, on May 22, I went to Eugene, Oregon, to run a women's 10,000-meter exhibition track race staged (thanks to Janet Heinonen) at the site of the men's Olympic Trials Marathon race. I chose to drive instead of fly, and that was another poor judgment call. I picked up food poisoning en route and again had a terrible race. In hindsight, the combination of all those events within a month's time was entirely ill advised.

Peg Neppel and Carol Cook, teammates at Iowa State, both went under the American record (previously Cook's) in the Eugene race. Neppel won in 34:19.0 and Cook ran second in 34:42.2. My former teammate Cheryl Bridges finished third, then Nadia Garcia of San Diego finished just ahead of me.

Upon finishing this race, Cheryl was quoted as saying, "We need more of these [track races longer than 3000 meters], just to learn how to run them. I have no idea how fast I can run [a 10,000]. Just look at me. Do I look tired to you?" I stated at the time, "If they're going to add just one distance [to the Olympic program] for women, it shouldn't be the 3000 or 5000. That's still catering to the miler types. They should go straight to the 10,000 or the marathon."

Other events that year had disastrous results for me. While at Lake Tahoe with the visiting Hunky Bunch family from Hawaii, I was scheduled to run some high mileage. I proceeded to do too much too soon, considering we were training at a high altitude. I developed altitude sickness, which ruined the rest of my trip.

Returning to Waldniel, West Germany, in the fall for another Women's International Marathon resulted in another poor performance (2:55 in eighth place). My running log indicated I was still recovering from illness just prior to the trip. The same held true for my return to Sao Paulo at the end of December, where I ran yet another bad race.

In retrospect I realize I must have been accepting too many invitations and running races too close together, with too much traveling. Perhaps being the world record-holder led me to believe I was Wonder Woman. I found out the hard way that when you are at the top of your game, it's a fine line you are straddling as you're vulnerable to falling over the edge.

The 1976 Olympic Games in Montreal came and went with no distance events beyond 1500 meters offered to women. Although my name was at the top of the world list for women's marathon times in 1974, 1975 and 1976, I am not saying I would, should or could have won an Olympic medal. However, I feel I ought to have had the opportunity to try.

At Montreal a young, talented Grete (Andersen) Waitz competed in the semi-finals of the women's 1500 meters (4:04.8), but did not advance to the final. In 1977, she won the 3000 in the first IAAF World Cup (8:43:50), and she won the World Cross-Country Championships. She twice set the world record at 3000 (8:46.6 in 1975 and 8:45.4 in 1976). It was clear even then that she would excel at longer distances.

If 1974 and 1975 were my peak performance years, I would say that 1976-1977 became transition years – from competitor to activist. The notion that I had about letter-writing and petitions having any effect on increasing running opportunities for women internationally was giving way to more assertive actions. As for my own racing, I was transitioning to

79

more fun events, longer events and what I called adventure running.

Women's exhibition 10,000 in Eugene, 1976 (from left): me, Cheryl Bridges, Carol Cook, Peg Neppel.

13. Teaming Up

All the world's a stage,
And all the men (and women) merely players.
They have their exits and their entrances,
And one man (or woman) in his (or her) time plays
many parts.

Shakespeare (adapted)

The year 1977 began in Brazil, having finished another
Sao Silvestre race. This time, as was true of a lot of
races in 1976, I ran a disappointing performance in
large part due to food poisoning. The same was true for
Ric Rojas, who was traveling with Tom Sturak and me.
We all spent some time in Rio de Janeiro before flying
back to Los Angeles together, staying in Topanga
before Ric returned to Colorado. What began as food
poisoning may have turned into influenza, and I was
recuperating until mid-January.

Since befriending the Chun family when I won the
Honolulu Marathon, Leal-Ann Reinhart and I were
honored when the family invited us to join their team,
the Hunky Bunch, to compete in the 140-mile Perimeter
Relay in February 1977. The race circled the island of
Oahu.

This was normally a locals-only race, and so we
were quite honored by the invitation and didn't think
twice about accepting. A team consisted of seven
runners, and ours included Jerold, Hingson, Daven, Joy
and June Chun plus Leal-Ann and me. We ran seven

times each, averaging approximately three miles per leg. The longest, however, was close to eight miles and inaccessible to vehicles. This leg went to the oldest boy, Jerold, who was an expert at trail running.

Every team calculated its own start time based on this leg of the race. We had to estimate the time it would take us to reach this part of the course in daylight. For the entire rest of the course, one of two team support vehicles would always follow our runner. Leal-Ann and I anticipated going off on another adventure, this time teaming up with the Hunky Bunch. What I could not have anticipated was the eventual teaming up with Tom post-race.

Here are journal entries depicting the trip:

FEBRUARY 2: Since we're leaving for Hawaii tomorrow morning, and probably resting the next couple of days, I didn't hesitate to run 11 [miles] rather than eight today, as I'm sure Leal and Tom intended. As long as it felt good, why not?

FEBRUARY 3: Arriving here after noon today, Leal and I were met by Hunky and June [Chun] and presented with beautiful flowered leis. We napped this afternoon, went on approximately an eight-mile run, enjoyed a delicious dinner and spent the evening relaxing. The relay is set for Saturday evening, promising to be a lot of fun for all.

FEBRUARY 4: After a good night's sleep I rose around 8 or 8:30 for a small breakfast. Then Leal and I walked a couple miles to do some shopping for things to make a special-request batch of my granola. First, both of us napped a couple of hours, ran about 6 P.M. for 40 minutes and had dinner. Tomorrow we fully intend to rest prior to the relay. Starting time is midnight.

FEBRUARY 5: After a small breakfast and later an enormous lunch, we mostly rested the day away. June prepared for her Junior Miss Pageant, and the rest of the Chuns prepared for our overnight adventure. Connie supplied enough food for an army. As it turned out, we could scarcely eat a thing 'til [the relay] was over.

Early on, the only potential disaster was when one station wagon broke down. Thank goodness we had another car. From then on, we settled into a routine, we each ran well, and nothing more went wrong.

There were so many beautiful sights – fields of pineapples and sugar cane, a huge rainbow at sunrise, lovely shorelines, beach coves and other panoramic scenery.

FEBRUARY 6: The relay itself began at midnight (for us) and was much more fun as soon as we began to catch teams who started earlier. It was pretty lonely before that, although there was one college team we had fun dueling with at first. (We ended up way ahead of them.)

I was pleased with the way I felt pretty strong throughout. Often, I averaged six-minute miles and better. I totaled seven legs of the relay, the first was 4.7 miles, the last 1.5, and in between, they were about 3.0 miles. Our overall place was seventh, and we won the mixed-team division in a good time of 14:00:23. Total distance was 134 miles.

FEBRUARY 7: I slept from 5:00 P.M. yesterday until 6:30 or so this morning with only one interruption when Tom called. In fact, I awoke to find myself still in the cut-off shorts and halter-top I was wearing yesterday. It was a deep sleep!

Leal and I did the touristy thing and went to the Polynesian Cultural Center, really worth one trip. I most appreciated the lesson in Hawaiian quilting. After,

we ran about five miles when we returned to the Chuns'
at 6 P.M.

FEBRUARY 8: Although we did no running today,
I'd say we had a workout. After flying to Maui, Leal
and I rented a car, drove to Haleakala, and hiked into
the crater, 2½ hours worth for about six miles. It was
not only spectacular scenery en route, but also a
splendid clear night for viewing the stars.

FEBRUARY 9: We hiked out of the crater in 2¼
hours after a long night's sleep. It was warm and
comfortable, surprisingly. We returned the car to the
airport and boarded an early flight "home" to the
Chuns back in Honolulu. This was to no avail, because
no one was available to fetch us from the airport. So we
took another walk with those packs on our backs. This
time, 1½ hours. Upon returning to the Chuns' house, I
ran for about five miles. My weight is down (no
wonder), lower than my arrival by three pounds.

FEBRUARY 10: A.M.: about a three-mile run.
P.M.: approximate distances, in a park, three-mile
warm-up, half-mile fresh tempo, 10-12 shakeups, half-
mile easy, 8 x 330 fresh speed, 5 x 220 good/medium,
half-mile easy, 15 x 100 shakedowns.

On this day, I made a decision to call Tom and
share one of Connie Chun's brainstorm ideas. During
the time we spent on the road during the Perimeter
Relay, the story of my recent trip to Brazil for the Sao
Silvestre race came out. I revealed that while in Brazil
Tom had proposed. We actually tried to get married
there. However, the U.S. consulate broke the news to us
that winding through the bureaucracy would take
weeks.

Hearing that, Connie started a campaign to host our
wedding in Honolulu. Her teasing turned to imploring,
until I decided to at least let Tom know what was being

discussed. To my amazement, he agreed and booked a flight to be there in a few days.

Back to my journal:

FEBRUARY 11: A.M.: 1 hour, 35 minutes running, 13 miles. After running in the morning, Leal and I continued making good use of the day, going first to Hunky's medical clinic for my pre-marital tests, and to the Ala Moana shopping center for some shopping. We relaxed on the beach afterward for a couple of hours before returning home.

Tonight, Chinese New Year celebrations began. We celebrated with a seven-course dinner in Chinatown, entertained by Lion Dancers and a lot of firecrackers. I was really pleased to meet the judge who will perform the informal ceremony.

FEBRUARY 12: Workout was sort of a fartlek, for maybe eight miles in about an hour. Warmed up 2½ miles plus 14 shakeups, and approximately 8 x 440 loops on top of Tantalus and finishing with some jogging and 14 shakedowns.

FEBRUARY 13: A.M.: two-hour run. P.M.: Chinese New Year dinner with Hunky's family. Tom arrived late tonight.

Even though we were married on Valentine's Day, it's no wonder that I always remembered the occasion as more about Chinese New Year.

FEBRUARY 14: Today, in Foster Gardens, we were married by Judge Andrew Salz. In attendance were the Chuns, the Fergusons, the judge and his wife, and of course Leal. She was the "best person" as well as the "chauffeuse."

What a splendid wedding! The gardens were beautiful, the weather warm and sunny, and lovely leis. I wore one of carnations and tuberose (from the Fergusons), one of maile leaves and strands of pikoki (from the Chuns), and a handmade wreath of flowers from Naomi Salz.

Most appreciated was the service given by Andy. He wrote a lovely, personal piece for the occasion, one to be cherished always.

Yes, there was a morning workout along the bike path with Leal and Tom this morning.

FEBRUARY 15: Thanks to friends of the Chuns, we had a nice beach house for accommodations on the North Shore, near Haleiwa, and we continued running every day until we returned to the Chuns for a reception, where we were joined by running friends on the island on our final day before returning to the mainland on February 17.

Upon returning home to Los Angeles, I cannot believe we actually went to San Diego for the Indoor Games on the 18th, staying with the Gookins. I ran with Thom Hunt on the 19th for eight miles. On February 20, my Tom was running the Culver City 30K District Championships, intentionally, while I was running it for a workout only. But somehow, despite my fatigue, I won in 2:02 (in 1976 it was more like 1:54, so not a serious effort in '77). I planned on doing about 6:30 pace, which worked out to about just that.

On one hand, we returned to life on the running circuit as we knew it. At the same time, however, we were beginning a new chapter of our lives. Tom was one of the most liberated males I knew. He not only supported my running; he supported my activism. I do not believe I would have been so strong throughout the struggle for equality, never mind the struggle of tough workouts and tougher races, had he not been at my side.

Tom Sturak (left) runs with me in a six-mile track race.

14. Races of Our Own

It takes all the running you can do
To keep in the same place.
If you want to get somewhere else,
You must run at least twice as fast as that.
      Lewis Carroll, "Through the Looking Glass."

In the early 1970s, women-only races were scarce. However, given the running boom of that decade and the passage of Title IX in 1972, opportunities grew quickly.

Race director Fred Lebow hosted the first women-only road race, the Crazylegs Mini-Marathon in 1972. The distance chosen was 10 kilometers, or about one-quarter the length of a marathon. This distance was deemed as more manageable, one that would ensure greater participation by women. Sponsors over the early years included L'Eggs and Bonne Belle. The race grew quickly from 78 participants in the first year to more than 2000 by the mid-1970s.

I ran my first New York 10-kilometer road race in an all-women's race, the AAU National Championships on May 18, 1974, and placed second. I was unaware of the Mini-Marathon that was held within weeks of this race. Fred Lebow picked me up from the airport on my first trip, and he explained to me how the Mini drew more participants than the Nationals, because a large number of women who ran were otherwise put off by the word "championships."

As an aside, I remember meeting Fred for the first time. He was living in a fifth-floor walk-up apartment, where he paid more to garage his little convertible Karmann Ghia car (like mine) than his rent. He always recalled meeting me, telling people that I was a "flower-child from California" in my bell-bottom pants, beads, knapsack (my backpack, actually) and bare feet. (I swear I was wearing Birkenstock sandals.)

I returned to New York City to run the Mini on May 10, 1975. In my whole running career, there are but a couple of races I would call "peak performances." This race was one of them. Out of the scores of women runners, I remember a lead group of about two dozen emerging in the early stages. Then at the four-mile mark Charlotte Lettis and I pulled away, side by side. True to what peak performances become, the move felt effortless. We drew strength from each other, pushing together toward the finish line.

I wondered for a moment if we were going to tie, but I decided that if Laszlo Tabori were there, he'd be yelling for me to make a move. So I did. And then Charlotte did too. I was no match for her sprint speed, and she beat me to the finish line. It was, however, a most gratifying race. Even she said afterward, "Wouldn't it be great if we had tied?" I'm just as glad we gave a competitive finish. I am more pleased that Charlotte and I have become lifelong friends.

In 1977, a Boston women-only race now known as Tufts began as the Bonne Bell Mini-Marathon. It was the culminating event of a series of 12 races across the country. The race directors expected perhaps 200 women and were overwhelmed with more than 2000 participants. Lynn Jennings won the inaugural 10K in 34:31. She went on to win six titles, and had five second-place finishes. The next year, 1978, Joan Benoit was the winner, setting an American record at 33:16. At its peak in 1983, the Boston Tufts race for women attracted nearly 9000 women participants.

I too was one of the Bonne Bell race directors, for the 1978 women-only 10K held in Beverly Hills. The race doubled as the national championships at that distance. Ruth Wysocki won that title, to go with her championship at 800 meters.

Other women-only races evolved during that decade: in Baltimore, Maryland, the Women's 10,000-Meter Run in 1977, and in Albany, New York, the Freihofer's Women's 5K and 10K in 1979.

In the history of the Road Runners Club of America, the period of 1973 to 1978 is entitled "The Renaissance." Jeff Darman's term as RRCA president (elected 1977) brought significant changes. One symbolic change: women runners were added to the organization's logo. In a more significant development, Darman advanced women's running through a newly formed RRCA committee headed by Henley Roughton (now Gabeau), who created the Women's Distance Festival, a series of women-only races.

In an even broader sense, Darman laid the groundwork for the running boom of the 1970s, including his lobbying efforts aimed at the U.S. Congress for the passage of the Amateur Sports Act of 1978. This act forever changed the nature of our sport for women and men in this country, disbanding the AAU and placed track and field, distance running and race walking under the governance of the Athletics Congress (TAC) and eventually USA Track & Field (USATF). The new federation was charged with a mandate to better serve, represent and be responsive to its athletes. Both Jeff Darman and Henley Roughton

Gabeau became valuable assets on the International Runners Committee in the near future.

Women-only races have continued to grow in the number of races offered and in the number of participants to this day. In fact, women now make up more than 50 percent of marathon participants, and an even bigger majority of marathoners run for charity causes in this country.

Start of the New York City Bonne Bell Mini-Marathon.

15. Years of the Women

*Of my two "handicaps," being female put more
obstacles in my path than being black. I've always met
more discrimination being a woman than being black.*
Shirley Chisolm, first black woman to serve in
the United States Congress

If I was influenced by the turbulent 1960s to question
authority, I was further influenced by the 1970s
feminist movement. The United Nations proclaimed
1975 the International Women's Year. As a result,
President Gerald Ford established a commission for its
observance in the U.S., and events were held over the
following two years. In 1977, more than 130,000
women attended state conferences across the country.

President Jimmy Carter appointed Bella Abzug to
preside over the culminating event in Houston, Texas,
which attracted more than 2000 delegates. A torch relay
originated in Seneca Falls, New York, with 3000
women carrying the flame to Houston. Texas
Congresswoman and Houston native Barbara Jordan
delivered the keynote speech. Dignitaries in attendance
included Lady Bird Johnson, Rosalyn Carter, Betty
Ford, Coretta Scott King and Billy Jean King.

According to the *Handbook of Texas*, "The
conference opened with a clear sense of purpose as well
as much fanfare... Although the National Women's
Conference was not a lawmaking body and could only
propose nonbinding recommendations, it was directed

to arrive at a national plan of action to help remove sex barriers and better utilize women's contributions." Proposals would be submitted to the President and Congress.

These lofty goals are what attracted my best friend, Leal-Ann Reinhart, and me to the conference. Leal-Ann was the reigning women's national marathon champion of 1977. We went seeking help for our cause on behalf of women runners with the objective of gaining Olympic inclusion for all distance-running events.

"Twenty-six major topics were considered by the delegates, including the ERA [Equal Rights Amendment], abortion, lesbian rights, child care, minority women, homemakers, battered women, education, rape, health and a cabinet-level women's department," the conference report stated. The enormity and importance of these issues empowered me and at the same time humbled me to the point that I felt fortunate I had rights to run at all, and perhaps was being somewhat selfish to ask for more.

What I could not anticipate at the time were the future influences and activism of several women I met that week in 1977: Henley Gibble, Peggy Kokernot and Mary Cullen. On the occasion of the 50th anniversary of the Road Runners Club of America (RRCA), writer Jim Ferstle interviewed Henley (now with the last name Gabeau). Her comments:

"In 1977, Jeff Darman (then RRCA president) asked me to be the RRCA contact and liaison to the U.S. State Department for the International Women's Year torch relay that started in September in Seneca Falls, New York, and finished in Houston, Texas, in late November.

"I was to coordinate all of the running clubs, women and logistics of the RRCA participation, and

93

other stuff. It was a time when Bella Abzug, Gloria Steinem and Coretta Scott King would amble in and out of the office as I sat with a phone glued to my ear, in awe of these women.

"I was sent to Houston to organize the last week, where I met Jacqueline Hansen and Leal-Ann Reinhart... who were there to lobby for the inclusion of a women's marathon in the Olympics. It was that meeting that sent me back to Jeff Darman in the fall of 1977 with a mission: to have the RRCA be a force in that effort."

Darman promptly appointed Henley chairwoman of the RRCA's Women's Distance Committee. She became a tireless advocate for women distance runners, hosting speaking events and the RRCA Women's Distance Festival of races across the nation. She and I joined efforts as members of the International Runners Committee, starting in 1979.

Peggy Kokernot was the amazing young woman who picked up the torch relay in the state of Alabama, where Phyllis Schlafly of the "Stop ERA" movement had urged Alabama women not to support this feminist organization event. There was a 16-mile stretch left vacant of runners that marathoner Peggy was asked to cover. She did and saved the torch relay from being stopped in its tracks. Her picture on the cover of *Time* magazine, combined with her winning the Houston Marathon shortly after the convention and the strength she found after experiencing the conference, opened opportunities she never dreamed of before, according to her mother, Edith Grinell.

Peggy introduced me to Mary Cullen at the Houston conference. Mary's influence is felt in two seemingly separate worlds, as a long-distance runner actively competing in masters races and as a philanthropist who supports athletics and is a major patron of the arts. We spent a memorable journey together in 1987 when I was the U.S. head coach and Mary the U.S. team manager on a trip to Japan for the International Women's Ekiden competition in Yokohama.

In retrospect, I am pleasantly surprised at the effect this Houston conference had, not only for me but also for each of my friends. The seeds were sown, and the years ahead were full of action. This "child of the sixties" had become a "feminist of the seventies."

At the National Women's Conference in Houston (from left): me, Peggy Kokernot, Leal-Ann Reinhart, Mary Cullen.

16. Going Longest

Long may you run.
Long may you run.
Although these changes have come
With your chrome heart shining in the sun
Long may you run.

Neil Young

After winning the 1978 Revco Cleveland Marathon, I extended my racing distance to 50 miles for the first time, winning the U.S. championship and garnering 11 world records at intermediate distances. The race, directed by my husband Tom Sturak, took place on the track at Santa Monica College.

Yes, I said on the track, as in 200 laps on the dirt surface. Rich Benyo, editor of *Runner's World* at the time (and now editor of *Marathon and Beyond* magazine), wrote his highly detailed and highly entertaining account of the night in his "50 Miles By Track" article. At least I think it's entertaining, even hysterical at times, but it's one of those stories that maybe you had to be there to appreciate.

For Tom and I, this was an annual event. It began one year when he attended a meeting at the local AAU offices for all track and field clubs in our region. At the meeting, duties for staging the various regional championship races were divided among the local running clubs. As the representative for his club, and arriving late to the meeting, Tom was "volunteered" for whatever events were not claimed by the others – and thus was awarded the 50-mile championship.

After a couple of years hosting the event, he became sort of intrigued – or maybe the word is obsessed – with staging the event. Guilty by association, I was part of the race committee. I guess you could say we two *were* the race committee. This went on for a few years, and the hours were tough. Being the first to arrive and the last to leave made for a long day, starting in the afternoon and continuing past midnight.

One year it dawned on me that if I was a participant, I'd have shorter hours. I could actually leave when finished running. What a concept! All kidding aside, though, I suppose the real explanation was that I was intrigued by runners competing at 50 miles in the same way I was intrigued while watching my first marathon. That turned out well, so why not try this?

One obvious answer comes to mind. Fifty miles is as different from a marathon as the marathon is from the 10K. That's why not. But as my coach, Laszlo Tabori, always said of me, "You're the most stubborn runner I've ever met." And, "There are some things you have to find out for yourself."

Laszlo called me "stubborn" (I preferred "determined") when I asked to run my first marathon. So here we went again. However, unlike that marathon debut, this time I planned ahead and was well prepared – well, up to a point. As Rich Benyo put it, I was a two-time world record-holder in the marathon, so even though it was my first ultramarathon, I was far from inexperienced.

My strategy in training was similar to the marathon, only now multiplied by two. Instead of my longest runs being 20-milers, I built up to 40-milers. Rich wrote that he had seen me with Leal-Ann Reinhart running

97

through the San Francisco Marathon, as a mid-section to one of my training runs of 32-plus miles. It's true, I did use more than one marathon for a workout. This provided me a lot of company on my long run of the week.

My secondary goal in going up to 40 miles in training also had to do with something I'd observed over the years with ultra runners. It seemed that the "wall" that comes at about 20 miles in the marathon was actually more like 35 miles in the 50. Also this wall in the 50-mile appeared more profound, like a total personality change, a meltdown that was both physical and psychological.

Never having studied kinesiology or exercise physiology or any science that could define it, it simply made sense when I was told that the body used up all the glycogen it could store by 35 miles and was converting to burning fat. During this transition, one would naturally just slow down.

As an example, it was pointed out to me that the women, who inherently carry more body fat than men (in general, anyway) tend not to slow down as much. In fact, one runner, Eileen Waters, year after year seemed to prove this theory correct. She sped up at this transition point, averaging a faster pace than most of the men on the track in the latter stages of the race. So it seemed important to me to train my body to work through that 35-mile point in training.

One of my adages is that the marathon is the one event where you can do all your homework and still not pass the test, due to things beyond your control. The takeaway message is to go into the marathon as close to 100 percent as possible. This holds true for the ultra... times two.

In the race, I was doing just fine at the start. Rich Benyo wrote that I ran as if hooked to some fantastic clock. I did feel comfortable with the seven-minute mile pace as I clicked off the laps. Judges and timers were stopping watches and signing off on officially recognized distances as I broke a string of records (11 in all). What Rich may not have known was that the first thing to go wrong was my lap counters missed two laps, so all those records were a half-mile too long.

This was discovered by 50K, about the time I was falling into that wall, that abyss of the unknown, and I checked with my lap counter to find out how far my pace was slipping. For me to ask meant something was seriously wrong. It was going so badly, my counter asked my husband if she should even tell me. Tom said that if I had the mind to ask, then give me the time.

When this woman told me the lap split, I uncharacteristically snapped, telling her that I could not do that math and just give it to me in minutes per mile. She did, and it was nine minutes per mile. Suddenly I could do the math just fine, because I realized how much longer I was going to be out there. I stopped dead in my tracks and almost wept. Then I collapsed on the infield of the track right where I had stopped.

The officials and Tom had pored over my splits, found two laps missing and informed me that I could either take an average time to make up for the missing laps, but they wouldn't be official, or I could take the times that they officially recorded, because they were certified world track records.

At that point, I stood to set 11 of them: 20 kilometers, 1:30:41; 15 miles, 1:48:17; 25 kilometers, 1:52:02; 30 kilometers, 2:14:04; 20 miles, 2:23:52; 35 kilometers, 2:37:50; 40 kilometers, 3:00:41; 25 miles,

3:01:50; marathon, 3:11:50; 30 miles, 3:45:47; 50 kilometers, 3:51:01.

No question, I had broken the records. However, I would not be allowed to keep them unless I finished the race. Therein lay the problem. Rich Benyo wrote correctly about how dead my legs felt at that moment. It took a herculean effort to lift my knee to take a stride. What I needed was a cheerleader and not the sympathy my friends, the lap counters, were offering. My mood was so low that I took every suggestion as a command. Want to lie down? Okay. Want to drink something? Okay. Heck, if they asked me, "Want to commit hara-kiri?" I might have contemplated that too.

Fortunately, my coach and doctor both arrived together and yelled at me, "Get up and move. Your legs are going to cramp lying in that wet grass." I said okay. I re-entered the track exactly where I stepped off. And I finished at that same monotonously slow pace, but a half-hour had slipped by that was lost forever. Rich Benyo was right about that too. I would've continued breaking records had I just walked instead of stopped. I still won the overall championship title, in a time of 7:14:58. I did not get the 50-mile world record, but could claim all the others set en route.

Within a month following the 50-miler, I went to Minneapolis to run a 15K race, to Boston to run an eight-miler and 10-kilometer race in consecutive weeks, then the fourth week I ran the New York City Marathon. Apparently I did not learn my lesson from poor planning in 1976.

In the 1978 national 50-mile championship, run on a track in Santa Monica, California. Writer Rich Benyo is the runner on the right.

17. Grete the Great

Tenderness and kindness are not signs of weakness and despair, but manifestations of strength and resolutions.
Kahlil Gibran

World record-holder Christa Vahlensieck, of West Germany, and I rode together to the start of the 1978 New York City Marathon. On the bus, she told me that Grete Waitz was our competition that day. I said, rather surprised, "The 3000-meter World Cup champion?" Christa let me know that Grete had recently run a 16-kilometer cross-country course in under an hour. She added that Grete worked out hard, every day, twice a day.

(This conversation sounds simple enough, but you have to know that I didn't speak any German and Christa was not fluent in English. So this conversation probably took the entire bus trip in a game of charades.)

During the course of the race, what I previously perceived to be a small injury to my foot worsened dramatically. I thought it had only been a stone bruise from running on the tow-path in Washington, DC, just days before arriving in New York. With the pre-race rest and easy days, I didn't notice the sore foot too much.

Parts of the New York course require running over steel-grated bridges. Carpeting was laid with the best intentions, but from my vantage point it was simply too crowded to set foot on the carpet, so I was left to

102

running on the steel grating. I suspected at the time that one of my metatarsal bones fractured (which was later confirmed). I wanted terribly to stop, and at the point where we came off the bridge I thought I could walk to the finish line if I cut across Central Park. However, the crowd of spectators was so thick, it was impossible to drop out.

I was on First Avenue before the crowds thinned enough to pull aside. When I did, I slipped off my shoe and was massaging the foot when I felt someone put an arm on my shoulder. I was looking down at another runner's foot with her shoe off too, and looked up to see Christa. We walked together back to the finish line area, which wasn't easy because everyone tried to steer us back onto the course. We realized we had to get rid of our bib numbers, especially since Christa's was number one and mine number two.

Sitting on a grassy knoll in Central Park, overlooking the finish line from a distance, we could hear race announcer Toni Reavis say that there was "no sign of Vahlensieck or Hansen," but an "unknown runner with number 2000-something is leading the race." We looked at each other and said, "Grete!"

We watched her cross the line, breaking the world record, Christa's record. I saw tears well up in Christa's eyes, and it was my turn to put my arm on her shoulder, looking for the right words. I said something that Chantal Langlace (the woman who broke my record) once said to me: "You are a great runner. You had better days before, and you will again." For now, Grete had arrived, and she would change the women's marathon world forever.

Grete Waitz was by far the most accomplished female distance runner this world has ever known, and she transcended even those astonishing achievements

103

with her personality. She was the most gracious and dignified person I have known, the epitome of goodness and integrity. I am pleased and proud to have known her, to be a colleague, but mostly to call her a friend.

I don't believe many people realize that she also took an active role as an advocate for women distance runners and our right to run in the Olympics. I want to tell that story, because it's important and because I will be eternally grateful to her for generously giving her time and presence to this cause.

In 1979, I was pregnant with my first (and only) child, and did not run the New York City Marathon. However, I did run the Lasse Viren 20K Invitational cross-country race in Sycamore Canyon near my home. Grete won handily that day. I was running comfortably, in accordance with doctor's orders, and still placed fifth.

I suspect I may have talked to Grete about our recent respective trips to Montreal, where the International Runners Committee (IRC) met for the first time and the World Cup Track and Field Championships took place. Grete, defending champion from the 1977 World Cup, placed second in the 3000 meters. The IRC was established as a lobbying organization to seek all the distance runs for women in the Olympic Games. She very much supported the IRC cause, and eventually became our spokesperson.

Grete's victories and records are well recorded: nine New York City Marathon wins, five world cross-country titles, two London Marathon wins and one at the Stockholm Marathon, two world records for 3000 meters, 1500-meter Olympian, World Championships marathon win, and so on.

She broke 2:30 for the first time by any woman in her second NYC victory and ran under 2:30 for all her

104

remaining victories there. I recall the day she set that 1979 record of 2:27:33. I was at a trade show for running apparel, and over the loudspeakers came the announcement of the male winner. It was frustrating to wait to receive the news of Grete's earth-shaking performance. Roberto Quercetani (European editor for *Track & Field News*) called it "the most advanced of women's achievements." Here is a summary of his comments, as edited by Joe Henderson in the IRC Newsletter:

"A time such as Grete's would have been good enough to earn a medal in an (all-male) Olympic marathon as late as 1956. In terms of records, it was only in April 1935 that a male marathoner ran a bit faster than that. The Norwegian teacher thus appears to be 44 years behind the male clock. Before we regard this as a long lapse of time, let's consider the situation in other events. Women trail men by nearly 80 years at 100 meters, and more than that at 400, 800 and 1500.

"It's in the distance events that the 'history gap' becomes decidedly narrower. Lyudmila Bragina showed the way in 1976 with her 8:27.2 3000, a mark first surpassed by a male runner in 1926. That man, mind you, was Paavo Nurmi. Grete Waitz has gone further than any other woman athlete with her marathon record. That's why we referred to it as the most advanced of women's achievements in the sport."

Norway joined in the boycott of the 1980 Moscow Olympics. Lobbying efforts by the IRC and many others succeeded in the International Olympic Committee announcing in early 1981 that the women's marathon would be added to the 1984 Olympic program in Los Angeles. The first-ever World Track and Field Championships were held in 1983 in Helsinki. Grete won the marathon, and Mary Decker Slaney won the

1500 and 3000 meters. Both women served as spokespersons for the IRC at the press conference in Helsinki to announce the international class-action lawsuit against the IOC for the orphaned events, the 5000- and 10,000-meter races.

Some say the only missing award in Grete's achievements is the Olympic gold medal. In 1984, she earned a silver behind Joan Benoit Samuelson. Ever the gracious person, she made no excuses, although a few of us knew she was wearing a back brace and was undoubtedly in pain. She simply said that Joan was the better runner that day.

In 1988, Grete was unable to finish the marathon at the Seoul Olympics, pulling out at 18 miles with a knee injury. Her last marathon came in 1992, accompanying New York City Marathon director Fred Lebow the year he turned 60 and after his diagnosis of brain cancer. It took them over 5½ hours to complete the distance. She told me it was the hardest thing she ever did.

We kept in touch over the years, if only by phone and e-mail. One conversation I recall came when she was getting back to an exercise routine while undergoing cancer treatment, and she described her week of workouts on the treadmill. I replied that she was way ahead of me and I was feeling lazy (thinking that I only suffered arthritis).

To me, the memory of Grete is not the count or color of her medals. She transcended the accomplishments with her integrity, her grace and her dignity. Grete was without controversy, as fellow IRC member Janet Heinonen pointed out to me upon hearing of her death in 2011.

Grete Waitz is our heroine and always will be. She was brave and courageous throughout life, and is sorely missed. May she rest in peace.

With Grete Waitz at the 1979 Lasse Viren
run in Malibu, California, when I was
pregnant.

18. New Adventures

Of all the rights of women,
the greatest is to be a mother.

Lin Yutang, Chinese writer

As my next new racing adventure, I entered the Catalina Marathon in 1979. Leal-Ann Reinhart did not join me in this venture, but her husband ran with me. Here is how that came about.

My first contact with this race came in 1978 when Nike sponsored it. Tom Sturak now worked for Nike, and we were on a race committee to provide a 10K race in the town of Avalon. The 10K was accessible to a larger number of runners who were not up to the challenge of the marathon but could enjoy the trip to Catalina Island. The 10K was run entirely within the confines of the town, and on streets, and took place on Saturday.

This was smart planning, as it provided a large audience for the finish of the marathon the next day, Sunday morning. There was a connection with the Topanga 10K, in my hometown, because the winners there received a free trip to run Catalina. I did not run the race that year, but I got my workout in both days by covering all of Avalon, plus the beachfront and some of Wrigley Gardens. It was a fun weekend with the races, a barbeque afterward and dinner with dancing at the casino.

When I returned to Catalina in 1979, it was to work the 10K again but to also run the marathon with Michael Reinhart. We arrived in Avalon by boat late Friday night, delayed in Long Beach due to engine trouble. After working at Saturday's 10K, I got up at 4:30 the next morning to take a boat to Cherry Cove for the start of the marathon.

Michael and I ran the whole way together, including hurdling over a rattlesnake at mile 23 while we were running downhill in rapid descent toward the finish line in Avalon. The entire course was made up of fire roads and dirt trails with beautiful scenery the whole way. There were buffalo and wild boar, plus that one rattlesnake. At one point in the course, we could see the ocean on both sides of the island.

The spectacular course was not unlike the trails I ran at home over the Santa Monica Mountains. I felt right at home and at ease as we coasted along at about an eight-minute-mile pace for a finish time of 3:26 (a women's course record). The finish was emotional, coming into town to a cheering section made up of spectators and 10K runners. It was so much fun.

My last marathon of the year was back in Waldniel, West Germany, where I was unable to finish. At the time, I had no clue why. I simply ran out of energy by 18 miles and collapsed with chills. Joan Ullyot, for whatever reason, suspected I was pregnant. This was confirmed after we returned to the States, upon my doctor's examination.

I kept running through my pregnancy, under the guidance of my doctor. She advised that while she wouldn't approve her other patients taking up running, this was something I had always done, and to tell me to stop would be detrimental to me. She did ask me to scale back and consider these criteria: don't let my heart rate get too elevated, stay aerobic, stay hydrated, don't allow my temperature to go to extremes, cold or hot, and be alert for any body, muscle, tendon or ligament changes, particularly bleeding.

Observing these restrictions, I ran fifth behind Grete Waitz in a local race, the Lasse Viren 10K trail run in Sycamore Canyon, Ventura. I placed ninth in another run, the Susan B. Anthony 10K Freedom Race in Tucson, Arizona. There I met Hattie Babbitt, the wife of Arizona's governor, along with a woman dressed up as Susan B. Anthony, at post-race ceremonies. I was always completely aerobic in my pace, but the women finishing ahead of me and behind me were nonetheless surprised.

Tom directed an international all-women's race, the Twentieth Century Fox Marathon, designed to follow the 1932 Olympic Marathon course in Los Angeles. I had done some publicity for the Fox studios, including appearances with then-mayor Tom Bradley.

However, under the circumstances of my pregnancy, I simply watched from the sidelines and on the press truck. Bev Shingles, of New Zealand, won the race in 2:45:46. The following day, I went to the Hollywood Park horse track to watch Grete Waitz win a 10K race easily in 32:35.

The next marathon Tom directed was Las Vegas. Actually we were co-directors, but upon arrival I caught a horrible case of influenza and was rendered rather useless as a worker. It was great to be reunited with my good friend Eleonora Mendonca, from Brazil. She came to run in Las Vegas on her return trip from the Tokyo Women's Marathon. She brought not only news of great race results, but also an encouraging report.

Ellie was invited to participate in the Tokyo race, the first sanctioned by the IAAF. She said she was honored to take part, but did not know at the time she would witness history in the making. IAAF President Adriaan Paulen attended, and in his speech he made it clear that he fully supported participation of women in the marathon and declared he would lobby to include this event in the Los Angeles Olympic Games. Joyce Smith, who had won the international marathon in Waldniel eight weeks prior, won the Tokyo race in 2:37:48. Ellie ran 2:58:25, and a total of 20 women from nine countries broke three hours.

February brought the rainstorm of the decade (if not the century) to my hometown of Topanga. People still refer to it as the "flood of 1980." There was so much rain, the creek overflowed and undermined our road. Mudslides closed several stretches of this road, the only way in and out of our canyon, essentially stranding us in our homes with no power or running water. Eventually, Tom and I evacuated by donning backpacks and knee-length boots, hiking out of the canyon to a point where some friends could collect us. At nearly seven months pregnant, I needed to keep my appointment with my doctor, and since we were "out" we went ahead to San Diego for the indoor track meet.

In March, I participated as a guest speaker at a women's distance running camp in Gainesville, Florida. Ann Gill created this unique event, with a great agenda and the best meals ever offered at any camp. By April, in between childbirth classes, I caught the news of the Rosie Ruiz cheating scandal at the Boston Marathon – an injustice to the true winner, Jacqueline Gareau of Canada.

Then, finally, came May and the birth of my son Michael. As a nurse referred to the experience as another chapter in my book, she could never have known how prophetic her statement became. As for me,

111

this child of the sixties, turned feminist of the seventies was on her way to becoming a soccer mom of the eighties!

At the 1981 Catalina Marathon with Belle Foster (left) of me, Jack Foster, John Brennand and an unidentified man on the right.

19. Making It Official

Never doubt that a small group of thoughtful,
committed citizens can change the world; indeed, it's
the only thing that ever does.
Margaret Mead

Despite increasing opportunities for women distance runners on the home front, the international governing bodies were not picking up on the trend. A key turning point came at Nike headquarters in Beaverton, Oregon. Nike executives, particularly those in running promotions and specifically Rob Strasser in marketing, listened to the concerns of women distance runners, taken to them by Nike's newly assigned masters athletes representative, my husband Tom Sturak.

Early in 1979, Nike ran a magazine advertisement in several major running publications, chiding the International Olympic Committee for its rejection of women distance runners and asking for reader response. This ad campaign was the brainchild of Pam Magee, Nike women's athletic representative. Literally thousands of supportive letters were received.

Consequently, Nike began to investigate ways it could implement a long-term financial commitment in support of a strong and effective lobbying effort to help women distance runners gain entry into the Olympic Games. Meetings took place with Tom and me, Rob Strasser, Pam Magee and Nelson Farris. Joe Henderson was asked to write a preliminary proposal, then to work with Tom and me to form a committee. We met in April 1979 to prepare a second draft of the proposal and to plan an organizational meeting.

The International Runners Committee consisted of the "movers and shakers" in the running community, with the common goal of lobbying international governing federations to include women's distance races in the Olympic Games program. Original members of the executive board included Joe Henderson, executive director; Eleanora Mendonca (Brazil) and myself, co-presidents; Jeff Darman, Doris Brown Heritage, Nina Kuscsik, Leal-Ann Reinhart, Henley Roughton (Gabeau), Manfred Steffny (West Germany), Tom Sturak, Joan Ullyot, Ken Young, Sarolta Monspart (Hungary), Lyn Billington (England), Arthur Lydiard (New Zealand) and Miki Gorman (Japan).

The executive committee met formally for the first time in August 1979 in Montreal at the World Cup Track and Field Championships. The objectives were few, and the focus was very specific. We would push first to eliminate inequality by expanding the women's distance running program in the Olympic Games by 1984, with particular attention to the marathon but also to adding the 3000-, 5000- and 10,000-meter races. Other objectives addressed initiatives that would support the first objective: to include the women's and men's marathon, 5000 and 10,000 in the World Cup and the newly proposed World Championships to begin in 1983. (The World Cup already had the 3000-meter race.)

We met next in January 1980, in San Francisco at the home of member Joan Ullyot. Guest speaker was Michael Harrigan, who previously headed the Presidential Commission on Olympic Sports, which evolved into the Sports Act passed by Congress in 1978. He presented an historical perspective of women's involvement in Olympic sports. It was clarified that new events or changes would have to go through the IAAF's Women's Committee, then to the Technical Committee, which, if convinced, would make recommendations to the International Olympic Committee.

The IRC continued to monitor growth and progress of the women's marathon internationally. We took every opportunity possible for lobbying efforts. Doris Brown Heritage was subsequently sent to attend the next IAAF Technical Committee meeting to lobby on our behalf.

The Technical Committee did vote in favor of a women's marathon. IAAF President Adriaan Paulen personally delivered the recommendation to the IOC Program Commission (an Olympic consulting group responsible for sifting through the requests for new events). The Program Commission inexplicably concluded that "more information, more medico-scientific research and experience need to be achieved." The IRC telegraphed the IAAF to urge the IOC to overrule the Program Commission's rejection or delay final action. Paulen appealed repeatedly on behalf of women before the IOC Executive Committee.

Several factions supported the women's marathon. We hoped the Women's Committee chair, Maria Hartman, would put forward a request for inclusion of all women's distance events, but she failed to do so. As the marathon came close to a vote at meetings in Moscow in 1980, our inside information came from Robert Giegengack, member of the USOC. He informed us that because of the U.S. boycott of the 1980 Olympic Games in Moscow, the Eastern Bloc

115

countries were predicted to vote against any proposal (i.e., the marathon) emanating from the West. Giegengack was instrumental in obtaining a postponement of the vote on the marathon until the committee next convened, in February 1981, in Los Angeles.

Los Angeles Olympic Organizing Committee President Peter Ueberroth, speaking through correspondence with his committee member Dick Sargent, replied to an advance notice that the women's marathon was about to be included in the 1984 Olympic Games. He stated that he could not accommodate any additional events or athletes, refusing any expansion of the program. Harry Usher, executive vice-president and general manager of the LAOOC, insisted that the number of athletes coming to L.A. for the Games must be controlled.

This statement drew numerous protests, most notably by Robert Giegengack. In May 1980, the LAOOC still stood firm against adding any new women's events. By then, a women's marathon had gained written support from Los Angeles City Supervisor Kenneth Hahn. Another boost came from USOC member Giegengack, who wrote in *New England Runner* that "track and field... is the number one Olympic sport. To tell us to run without women in a given event is like telling a baseball team to play without a second baseman because it costs too much." Giegengack proposed a resolution that the LAOOC enthusiastically support a women's marathon if the IOC agreed to the addition of the event. The proposal was passed unanimously.

Once again it seemed that the women were out – and this at a time when demonstration sports like baseball were being considered seriously for inclusion.

At the Moscow meetings, the IAAF took some firm steps forward. It recognized 5000 and 10,000 meters as official world-record distances. It established that the IAAF World Championships in Helsinki in 1983 would include a women's marathon. The 3000 meters and the 400-meter hurdles were added to the Olympic program as new women's events.

Telegrams flew back and forth from the International Runners Committee on the unresolved question of the Olympic marathon. Whether it was jeopardized by a backlash of officials angered over the U.S. boycott of the 1980 Moscow Olympics or because more important matters took precedence is unclear, but the women's marathon nearly became a dead issue. It was revived by the intervention of IAAF President Paulen and the now-enthusiastic support of the LAOOC.

Shortly before the Los Angeles meeting in 1981, confronted by the inexorable fact of another world record by Grete Waitz and a growing international clamor for justice, the IOC's general membership took long-awaited action. It reversed the Program Commission's recommendation not to add a marathon for women to the 1984 Games, opened the matter for reconsideration and delegated authority to its nine-member Executive Board. In the last week of February 1981, almost a century after the idea was first proposed by a Greek runner, Melpomene, the Executive Board of the IOC made it official: the women's marathon would be added to the roster of Olympic events in 1984.

By the time the decision came down, it was not news to any of us on the International Runners Committee, so the announcement was somewhat anti-climactic. In my mind we were already moving forward to the next campaign – to win acceptance for the now-orphaned events, the 5000 and 10,000.

Cover of a brochure from the International Runners Committee brochure.

20. Pressing Our Case

Disobedience is the true foundation of liberty.
H.D. Thoreau

With the women's marathon now joining the Olympics in 1984, the 5000- and 10,000-meter races remained left off that program. The International Runners Committee's focus turned to these events, but without the support of the IAAF there appeared to be no chance of adding them. In brief, the president and secretary of the federation told me personally that, despite having satisfied all the prerequisites for inclusion, this wouldn't happen for these "boring" events that would not "sell tickets at the gate."

The American Civil Liberties Union (ACLU) completed a study it commissioned to assess women's participation in the Olympic Games, reporting that women had access to only one-third the number of events the men had available to them. The ACLU director in Los Angeles, Ramona Ripston, then threatened legal action against the IOC.

I heard her discuss this in a 1980 radio interview, and I contacted her to offer my support. Although it appeared that the IOC was mending its ways by adding the women's marathon, I informed the ACLU of the blatant discrimination and omission of the 5000 and 10,000. We met, and I was sent on a mission to see if I could prove that women runners satisfied the rules for adding new events.

I did not know if the ACLU expected never to hear from me again or if it was testing my resolve, but I took up the challenge. With Nike's assistance and resources, we, the IRC, were able to obtain signatures on right-to-sue letters from nearly 80 women in almost 30 countries, representing the top world-ranked women in the 5000 and 10,000. The letters had gone out in 10 different languages to these women on every continent.

Attorney Susan McGrievy offered to take on our case. A former long-distance swimmer, she was compassionate to our cause. On August 10, 1983, the lawsuit was filed in Los Angeles. The announcement was made with ACLU lawyers on August 11, on NBC television's "Today Show" in Los Angeles and simultaneously at a press conference hosted by Nike at the first World Track and Field Championships in Helsinki. There I was with fellow IRC member Eleonora Mendonca, joined by Mary Decker, fresh off the medal stand for her 1500 and 3000 wins, and Grete Waitz, the marathon winner. They served as spokespersons at our press conference before worldwide media.

Defendants included the International Olympic Committee, United States Olympic Committee, International Amateur Athletic Committee, The Athletics Congress, Los Angeles Olympic Organizing Committee and Los Angeles Memorial Coliseum Commission. This unprecedented suit alleged that the defendants violated the Unruh Civil Rights Act, the federal Public Accommodation Act, the equal protection clauses under the U.S. Constitution and California Constitution, the Amateur Sports Act and international law prohibiting sex discrimination such as in the United Nations Charter.

Granted, it was difficult to name some of the defendants who included committee members sympathetic to our cause. For example, The Athletics Congress consisted of the Women's Long Distance Running Committee, which was certainly part of this fight. However, the lawyers explained that all parties involved had to be included in order to close all loopholes and any possibility of getting a run-around while seeking administrative remedies.

Additionally the international bodies, the IOC and IAAF, were adamant about protecting the integrity of the process, which angered me to no end since their almighty process was placed above the needs and desires of its constituents, the athletes. Besides, the "process" was whatever suited the IOC and IAAF, and was not enforced consistently, never mind fairly.

Consider IOC Charter Rules 32 and 33, regarding the process for adding new events. There were examples of new additions that did not meet these requirements. Furthermore, they were new *sports*, and we were only asking for new *events* within an already existing sport.

At least the age-old argument that women were not suited to run the 5000 and 10,000 was no longer an issue, since the marathon had been added. The most likely reason for not adding these two events was that they were not cost-effective. This is exactly what was told to me personally by Primo Nebiolo, the president, and Luciano Barra, the executive secretary, of the IAAF when they called the distance races "boring," and unattractive to ticket buyers. So the 5000 and 10,000 were never going to be included, as far as they were concerned.

This issue was perhaps the most outrageous of all. So that's why the marathon was added alone, because it represented television and ticket revenue? This statement alone sent me running to the ACLU, thinking lawsuit. As I saw it, we had exhausted all alternate options.

On March 6, 1984, the ACLU attorneys who represented 82 women long-distance runners, from 26 different countries on five continents, filed a motion for a default judgment in the lawsuit before Judge David Kenyon in Federal District Court in Los Angeles. They also asked for a preliminary injunction against all the defendants, including the LAOOC. In other words, it would compel the Los Angeles organizers to immediately add the 5000- and 10,000-meter events to the 1984 Olympic Games.

At the same time, a press conference was held in Eugene, Oregon, with spokespersons Mary Decker, Leann Warren, Cathie Twomey, Sissel Grottenberg (Norway) and myself. We maintained that the exclusion of the two events in question disenfranchised women distance runners worldwide, including those appearing with me in Eugene. I said, "Without the inclusion of these races in the 1984 Olympics, a whole generation of women runners will be denied the right to run for Olympic gold. All we want to do is to achieve parity with the men."

As one lawyer stated, "Up until 1983, Jacqueline Hansen and the IRC kept pushing within the system to get the middle-distance races, but no one within the system would take responsibility for what was requested. The bringing of the lawsuit was not done as a political statement, but was brought as a last resort because the plaintiffs felt there was no other solution for them."

In a 38-page decision, Judge Kenyon rejected the lawsuit on Monday, April 16, 1984 – news that I learned in a phone call in Boston, from *Los Angeles Times* reporter Julie Cart.

On June 8, ACLU lawyers argued their case in the Federal Court of Appeals in Los Angeles, after winning a motion to expedite an appeal before Judges J. Clifford Wallace, Harry Pregerson and Arthur L. Alarcon. The judges promised their ruling within a week.

Los Angeles Times Special Events Director Will Kern directed the U.S. Track and Field Olympic Trials in June 1984. He brought a sponsor, Etonic shoes, to the IRC to stage exhibition races in both the women's 5000 and 10,000. Although it was sad that these events were still controversial, I was very pleased Etonic stepped forward to make the races possible, and I agreed heartily to be the race director.

Ordinarily I would never pack the field with so many runners in any race on the track, but I was overwhelmed at the response from women runners and could not turn anyone away. Even assigning high standards to ensure quality races, there were nearly 30 runners in each race!

When the announcement was made in the stadium that these events would not be seen in the upcoming Olympic Games, you could hear the crowd booing the IOC and IAAF emphatically. Spontaneous cheering followed when the announcer offered that the women were running to make a statement.

Both races brought exciting performances. On June 17, Joan Benoit (Samuelson) was the decisive winner in the 10,000, finishing in the nation's fastest time to date (32:07) in front of 20,500 fans. The 5000 on June 24 was decided at the tape between Julie Brown (15:39.5) and Betty Jo Springs (15:39.7) before a crowd of 31,500, the largest audience of the entire trials.

It was ironic that reporter Marlene Cimons seated herself behind IAAF officials Nebiolo and Barra in the stands. Since she knew the whole backstory to the lawsuit, she leaned over to ask if they still thought the races were boring. (They pretended not to understand English.)

In between these two events, on June 22, the Federal Appeals Court judges ruled against the women runners, basically two to one. Judge Wallace stated that the Unruh Civil Rights Act, upon which our case was based, did not require "separate but equal events for women." This made no sense to me whatsoever, because it was not the women runners but the governing bodies that established gender-separated events throughout the Olympic Games events.

Judge Pregerson, who voted for us, countered, "If that were true, then there would be no requirement to have separate bathrooms in public libraries [for example]." If there was anything to be salvaged from the proceedings, it was the eloquent dissent written by Judge Pregerson. He began by quoting the founder of the modern Olympics, Pierre de Coubertin, who said the Games were meant to be an "exaltation of male athleticism" with "female applause as its reward." Pregerson concluded:

"The IOC made concessions to the widespread popularity of women's track and field by adding two distance races this year [3000 meters and marathon]. The IOC refused, however, to grant women athletics equal status by including all events in which women compete internationally. In so doing, the IOC postpones indefinitely the equality of athletic opportunity that it could easily achieve this year in Los Angeles.

"When the Olympics move to other countries, some without America's commitment to human rights, the

124

opportunity to tip the scales of justice in favor of equality may slip away. Meanwhile, the Olympic flame – which should be a symbol of harmony, equality and justice – will burn less brightly over the Los Angeles Olympic Games."

For the record, the 10,000-meter race for women was added to the World Track and Field Championships in Rome, 1987, and to the Olympic Games in Seoul, 1988. The 5000 replaced the 3000 at the 1995 World Championships, and the following year at the Olympic Games in Atlanta. The women's 3,000-meter steeplechase went on the program at the 2005 World Championships in Rome, and then into the Beijing Olympic Games of 2008. With these additions, the women's slate of distance events finally gained parity with the men's.

With Susan McGrievy at ACLU Annual Leadership Awards program in Los Angeles, 1984.

21. Mother on the Move

The best way to find yourself is to lose yourself in the service of others.

Mahatma Gandhi

In May 1980, I gave birth to our only child, son Michael. My journal from that year overflowed with news about him as I tried to capture every moment. My next journal began in October with this entry:

It's generally against my nature to begin a journal at a time other than the beginning of a year, or a season, but necessity warrants it. My last journal is so very full of a lot of memorable events, it's overflowing with extra pages stuffed in. What a year! The birth of a child is very special indeed. One would think I was the only mother in the world, the way I go on in words and photos and other collectibles. But it's an exceptional moment in my life, and I cannot say enough for it.

Michael, Tom and I flew to the New York City Marathon that October for me to do some interviews before and commentating during the race. I was there for Alberto Salazar's and Grete Waitz's spectacular winning performances that day (fastest marathon debut time for Alberto and another world record for Grete). Unfortunately, I'm not sure I was ever heard on the air since ABC had such technical difficulties trying to get its signal out amid all the skyscrapers of the city.

After the race, we enjoyed some time in Boston and Exeter, New Hampshire, where a Nike factory was located. New England is so beautiful in the crisp, cool weather of fall, with the changing colors of the leaves, is my favorite time of the year.

At the time, we were preparing for a move to Portland, Oregon. Tom left Los Angeles ahead of us, when he went from working part-time in the field for Nike to a temporary in-house position full-time. Michael and I followed in the spring of 1981, before his first birthday. Tom's stay there came during tumultuous times in the sport, beyond our campaign for women's running rights.

Unfortunately, despite well-placed protests, President Carter was perhaps advised badly and the U.S. team was forced to boycott the 1980 Olympic Games in Moscow. For a lot of athletes, this missed opportunity ended their Olympic dreams forever.

During Tom's tenure at Nike as director of running promotions, he fully supported the movement toward "above the table" professional prize money for road races. Don Kardong founded the American Road Racing Association (ARRA) with this mission in mind. The showdown with our federation came at the Cascade Run Off in Portland. This was summarized in a 2011 *Running Times* article by journalist John Meyer:

"What made the race a pivotal event in the history of the Olympic movement was what happened next. At the awards ceremony, the top finishers openly accepted prize money totaling $50,000, with $10,000 going to [male winner] Greg Meyer and also Anne Audain, the top female. Defiantly risking their Olympic eligibility, the rebel racers triggered a series of events that ultimately ended 'shamateurism' in distance running."

Initially, the outcome also caused a split in opinion, disqualifications from The Athletics Congress (TAC) and turmoil among America's runners. John Meyer added, "But the most significant effect of the Cascade Run Off rebellion was the way it fatally undermined the whole notion of Olympic amateurism. It was inevitable that the International Olympic Committee and its affiliated sport federations would allow professionals eventually, but there's no question who forced the issue."

Nike sponsored the World Veterans Track and Field Championships in New Zealand in January 1981, so Tom, Michael and I flew to Auckland in late December. One of Tom's athletes, Antonio Villanueva, also traveled with us to this competition for masters. After a brief stay in Auckland to rest up from the journey that shattered me, we drove some eight hours to our first destination, the home of Bev and Michael Shingles in Wanganui.

My first run was on a grass track – the site of Peter Snell's world-record mile, I was informed. Bev and Antonio both won a 10,000-meter race in Palmerston on January 3. Two days later, we all began the long journey south toward the Veterans Championships site in Christchurch. We arrived on January 6, and while I don't know now what possessed me to do it, I ran a slow 3000-meter race the next day, in 11:01. "Oh well," I noted, "I have a long way to go to get back in shape."

I enjoyed the trip through the beautiful countryside, crossing from the north to the south island by ferry, and I was pleased to attend a Shakespeare play while in Christchurch. We stayed about two weeks – just long enough for some of Michael's developmental breakthroughs, such as his first tooth coming in and learning to crawl.

On the journey back to Auckland, we stayed with Jack and Belle Foster in Rotorua, but only after another stopover at the Shingles' residence since the drive was so long. Rotorua was so beautiful! I called it a paradise, with lakes upon lakes, forests galore, green fields everywhere and thermal geysers steaming all over the place.

From Auckland, we took the 14-hour flight home. The return trip was so much more difficult with a baby who was mobile now (crawling fast and trying to walk). As well, he was cranky from teething, so who could blame him? Already he was becoming a world traveler.

During a visit to Oregon shortly before my move there, I ran through the 1981 Trail's End Marathon. I had asked one of Tom's employees at Nike to enter me, but he forgot and the race would take no late entries. I decided to run a 20-mile workout instead, but "finished" the marathon because I felt good.

Of course I did not cross a finish line but went off course to cross within sight of the finish clock. I could see that I ran 2:59:59. I am truly sorry that someone already took my picture in the lead farther out, because the poor woman who won unfortunately had my photo in the newspaper the next day. I am so sorry.

Pregnant in 1980, I did not compete in the Catalina Marathon. But I longed to return to this uniquely beautiful and idyllic, rustic race course, so I returned in 1981 to run it. I left the baby with my mother while I went over to the island. My track club teammate Dave Babaracki won the 10K. This time, I watched that race and left right after breakfast to take the boat to Cherry Cove, then hiked the 2½ miles to the campground for the overnight stay with the runners for the next morning's start of the marathon. In my journal, I referred to having "a good meal and good night's sleep at last." Any new mother will tell you about sleepless nights at home, and even a meal by campfire and a sleeping bag on the ground was an improvement.

130

Here is what I wrote:

Since this was to be my first comeback [marathon] race, I'd have to say it was a big success personally. I wanted to run it more than anything, to finish and to possibly better my PR for this course. I won, broke my own course record and enjoyed it as well. Oh, it was hard and took all the effort I could afford, but it was plenty worthwhile. What a satisfying experience! Charlie Vigil won overall in 2:37. The first five were under the course record. Jack [Foster] did great, running fourth in 2:44, enjoying it as much as I did. Missed Michael a lot.

Coincidentally, our son was born on Jack Foster's birthday, May 23. Jack and his wife Belle became good friends during those years. Jack and I had run the Honolulu Marathon together in 1975. A two-time New Zealand Olympian, he placed eighth in the 1972 Olympics in Munich, was silver medalist at the 1974 Commonwealth Games and finished 17th at the 1976 Montreal Games. At age 41, he set a masters world record of 2:11:19.

Jack stayed at our home several times and loved running the trails of Topanga. We also stayed at his home in Rotorua, New Zealand. Jack taught me to hose down my legs with cold water after our workouts, telling me if it was good enough for racehorses, it was good enough for us.

Jack had been a life-long bicyclist before he turned to running in his mid-30s. How sad, and somewhat ironic, that his death came when he was hit by a car while cycling in 2004.

The Fosters had traveled to Catalina with us for the 1981 marathon. Nike filmed the whole race, and the resulting production shows the beauty of the course that we enjoyed. Most of it can only be viewed by running or hiking through the otherwise closed-to-the-public grounds of the Conservancy.

It amazed me that I was still able to run just fine the next morning with friends – going over more hills, in fact. I have always maintained that running on dirt surfaces is gentler on the legs, and contributes to quicker recoveries, than races on the roads.

Also I have often looked back on that performance, wondering if there is some truth to the theory that post-pregnant athletes perform better with an added advantage of increased blood plasma levels, as some East German scientists purported. After all, I wasn't able to do long workouts, being a new mother, nursing and living in transition between homes, with little childcare support. So it wasn't the quality of my workouts that made for a good race. I still ponder this.

After this 1981 race, Belle and Jack returned to Los Angeles with us, and we enjoyed running in Topanga, Santa Monica and Venice. Their stay included a surprise going-away party – not for the Fosters, but for my family since Michael and I were about to join Tom in Portland.

I was very pleased about how well my running fitness was coming along. However, there were yet more complications to come.

*With son Michael at the Gale's Creek Marathon in
Oregon, 1981.*

22. "Allergic to Oregon"

To understand the heart and mind of a person, look not at what he has already achieved, but at what he aspires to do.

Kahlil Gibran

After my move to Portland, in the spring of 1981, Tom's new job kept him at the office or traveling seemingly all day every day. I felt elated to spend time at home with my son in his early years, but also a little lost without friends or family around me for support. In short, I missed running. Eventually, I identified a woman who offered childcare in my neighborhood where for an hour a day I could leave Michael with her and go for a run. As a new mother, I learned a new appreciation for my time to train and never wasted a moment.

We lived in Portland from spring of 1981 to December 1983. In that time, I had to adjust first to the rain and then to the cold weather. I did not own one piece of clothing with a speck of wool in it, so I increased my wardrobe considerably. I knew going in that it could rain 290 days of the year (who's counting?), and the skies could be overcast all the way from November to May. However, as much as I tried to wrap my head around these facts, my body wasn't having it.

I developed so many "colds," that I was on antibiotics 13 times in one year. Even in my first month in Oregon, I was going to the doctor's for a throat culture. Finally alarmed, I went back to Los Angeles to my own physicians and was diagnosed with allergies, the most serious one being to mold. Living in such a damp climate, it's hard to escape mold. I was just plain allergic to Oregon.

Eventually, I even had a diagnosis of candida to deal with as a result of being on so many antibiotics. The consequence was that not only did I first have to maintain a prescribed allergies diet, which was already very limiting; I also had to eliminate any foods that encouraged the growth of yeast (meaning no yeast products and no sugar of any kind).

The part I remember most vividly was the vile medicine I had to drink several times a day, a powder mixed with water, which tasted just awful. I simply put mind over matter, convinced myself there was no alternative and eventually came to think of it as lemonade and conquered that problem.

The ordeal of having so many "colds" in a year certainly dampened my training (pardon the pun). I know I had some pretty good races while in Portland, including the Rock Creek 10K, where I lived, and the Gale's Creek Marathon, which I won, if only with a mediocre time.

Living so far away from Laszlo Tabori, I was fortunate in that Tom Heinonen, the University of Oregon's women track and cross-country coach, agreed to coach me. I went to Eugene as frequently as I could, perhaps weekly, to see him. I loved running with his young women during cross-country season. They even invited me to run some of their collegiate races (unattached, of course), which was great fun. The highest compliment I received was when the women asked me if I had any eligibility left to join the team!

135

As a "Nike wife," I hosted many athletes who came through Portland, and we often entertained with dinner parties. Besides New Zealanders Jack and Belle Foster, and Bev and Mike Shingles, we also hosted Val and John Robinson once. All four of us, Tom included, ran a neighborhood race, the Rock Creek 10K, garnering a lot of awards among us.

We hosted Carl Lewis's birthday party (his 19th, as I recall). He visited frequently, and became my son's greatest hero. Carl was terrific with children and so inspiring to them. In later years, when I was heavily involved with youth sports, Carl would come speak to children at many of our events.

I also took on my first (and only) huge catering event during my tenure as "hostess" for Nike. They were opening new track and field promotions offices in Eugene and the director, John Gregorio, asked me to prepare food similar to the dinner parties I did at my home.

It still amuses me how I became a caterer, driving around grocery shopping on a mass scale, often parking alongside huge trailer-trucks with my little VW and my child in a baby-seat along with me. To add to the difficulties, I was preparing food in Portland to drive for two hours to Eugene to assemble. The logistics were crazy, but with John's and his wife Nancy's help, we put it all together for a successful party.

However, I never did anything quite like that again. On a smaller scale, I gave a bridal shower for Mary Decker in our home. But I quickly squashed any mention of catering the wedding. I had enough from that one Nike experience.

This is the kind of crazy schedule I was keeping at times: May 21 and 22, 1981, I went from Portland to Cleveland to speak on a panel of women runners for the

136

RRCA, hosted by Henley Gibble (Gabeau), Nina Kuscsik and Elizabeth Phillips. On May 23, I was back in Los Angeles to win the Tough Topanga 10K (a race which now bears my name) in my hometown with a 44:43 time. The next day, ran the Brentwood 10K directed by my dear friend Valerie Johnson, where I placed third in 37:33. From L.A., I flew directly to Portland to celebrate Michael's birthday. May 23, 1981, journal:

A year ago, it was a day of pain and trials, fatigue and stress, joy and love, thrills and emotions running high. All our expectations [were] fulfilled. It was wonderful. It was hard, too, my body going through some strange times. Tom thinks it's good and fitting I'm off running races a year later. Tomorrow I'm going home to my family. We'll put candles on the cake, blow up balloons and have the neighborhood kids over for a party. And I'll be with my two most loved ones again.

In the summer of 1981, I traveled with Tom on his European trip and for some reason chose to run the Enschede Marathon. Given the number of ailments and injuries I was dealing with, and all the chiropractor and physical therapists I was seeing, it was not a wise choice. I was unable to finish this race, and the attempt only worsened my physical condition.

We traveled to Dublin, en route to Oslo, for an international track meet. I spent some time with Grete Waitz, searching for Jacuzzis and spas to ease some of the pain. She, too, was suffering an injury and had to pull out of a track event.

We returned home in August, and on a happy note we enjoyed Shakespeare in Ashland, Oregon. But back to training, I was seeking new orthotics to add to the list of treatments. My major complaint was that my left leg thigh (hamstrings in particular) was beyond tight. It was

137

no doubt the beginning of a more serious injury to come.

Health issues did not only plague me. At one point, Michael got so sick (en route to L.A. for a speaking engagement I had to cancel) that he had to be hospitalized for dehydration. The following year, he was in the hospital twice, once for a cut he suffered in a fall, and on a separate occasion a scraped knee became so infected his lymph node swelled to the point of requiring surgery.

At the end of 1981, I wrote:

Well, like Leal-Ann [Reinhart] said the other day, let's hope next year's journal is filled with something other than injuries and doctors. I hope it's filled with good news, good health, good friends, good times.

When I returned to Catalina in 1982, the trip wasn't just 26 miles across the sea. I flew into L.A. from Portland, and Michael stayed with Grandma again. My journal reports that I drove out to the start in a truck the night before, over some of the marathon course. We scattered a couple of herds of buffalo along the way.

I was pleased enough that I was able to finish the marathon in the same time as my first attempt, 3:26, feeling in control the entire way. I suppose I wasn't in the best shape or I'd have been running track instead of doing a marathon, so I wasn't disappointed that I didn't break my course PR time that day.

In 1982, I enjoyed some lighter moments, whether it was Michael's first haircut or having a good race (winning a 30K race in Eugene). We continued to work constantly on the International Runners Committee matters, including a meeting of the whole committee in San Francisco. I also returned to the site of my best marathon, the Nike-OTC, where slightly older and slower I ran a respectable seventh place in 2:46.

The following year, 1983, Grete Waitz won the London Marathon, tying Allison Roe's world record with 2:25:29, while at Boston Joan Benoit (Samuelson) won Boston in 2:22:43. What an amazing weekend for the women's marathon!

Although I salvaged a few good races, like second at the Alaska Women's 10K Run and second at the Portland Viking Classic 8K, I was still struggling with nagging hamstring pain and a newly developed, yet again, metatarsal stress fracture.

All this time, I was doing IRC work, including big mailings, in preparation for the announcement of the IRC and ACLU lawsuit on behalf of the women's 5000 and 10,000 being announced at the World Track and Field Championships in Helsinki on August 11, 1983.

It was a heady time, going to the first World Championships for a press conference about the lawsuit and to watch the first women's marathon, as well as the first 3000-meter race. Unexpectedly, I was delighted to find an old friend who offered his support and accompanied me to the stadium for track events. Wilt Chamberlain told me how proud he was of what we were accomplishing. (He is someone I'd known from my earliest days on the track, where he attended most of our meets, with his San Diego-based club, Wilt's Wonder Women.)

Soon after my return from Finland, tests in Eugene and Los Angeles diagnosed compartment syndrome for those hamstrings, and surgery was scheduled for October 1983. The clock started ticking. It was just seven months to the Olympic Trials, and I had yet to obtain a qualifying time to enter. That deadline was just six months out.

Speaking at a Road Runners Club of America event.

23. Race Against Time

*We are in for a very, very long haul... I am asking for
everything you have to give. We will never give up...
You will lose your youth, your sleep, your patience and
your sense of humor, and occasionally... the
understanding and support of people you love very
much. In return, I have nothing to offer you but...
your pride in being a woman, and... all the dreams you
ever had for your daughters, and nieces, and
granddaughters... your future and the certain
knowledge that at the end of your days, you will be able
to look back and say that once in your life, you gave
everything you had for justice.*

> **Jill Ruckelshaus**, in a speech delivered at
> the National Women's Political Caucus
> 1977, California Convention

The year 1984 became the most dramatic of my entire
running career. It began in an attempt to rebound from
surgery, get back in running shape and obtain a
qualifying time to go to the first Olympic Trials
Marathon for women. This goal was my top priority.
I'd been trying to qualify for months but was stymied
by mysterious symptoms in an upper leg. I only
suffered them after a run lasting more than 45 minutes,
or about one-quarter of the marathon distance.

Fortunately for me, I had a brilliant orthopedist, Dr.
Jerome Bornstein, who figured out that I had
compartment syndrome of the hamstring muscle –

unusual but not so difficult to fix. In the process of diagnosing the injury, he sent me to find a doctor in Oregon (where we were then residing) to determine if the injury was related to nerve endings. It just so happened that I located a doctor in Eugene who, a good runner himself, had suffered this very injury.

Dr. Paul Raether assured me in September 1983 that the tests determined it was not a nerve conduction problem, but it was certainly compartment syndrome of the hamstring. He informed me his was one of the first two cases that he had seen reported in medical journals and that I would be the third.

He consulted with Dr. Bornstein, who tested me for compartment syndrome back in L.A. He performed surgery in November 1983. I then had until April to run a qualifying marathon better than 2:51:16 in order to compete in the U.S. Olympic Trials in May.

To my great relief, the recovery was not lengthy and did not require physical therapy. I was able to walk out of the hospital the same day, without crutches. I did have some issues with the spinal tap and had to return to the ER for a patch because a hole remained in my spine, where I was losing spinal fluid and thus the severe headaches every time I tried to get up from a lying position. I was running again within a week, as soon as the stitches, all 28 of them, were removed from the incision. I called that nine-inch scar on the back of my leg my "war paint," and I found it to be empowering.

My first attempt at qualifying came on February 19, 1984, at the inaugural Los Angeles International Marathon, directed by husband Tom with Jim Bush. I was trying to run with the least amount of effort, just fast enough to break the Trials standard. My leg began to cramp in the latter part of the race and I slowed too much, finishing in 3:04.

The next try was less than a month later, March 10, at the Los Alamitos Marathon, where I paced with a colleague from the Santa Monica Track Club. When I thought she sped up, I stayed at my pace, which unfortunately was slowing, and I missed the required time by just over two minutes (with 2:53:18).

In both races, nothing physically hurt, so my coach consented to one more try. I wouldn't advise anyone to run four marathons within four months, but this was an exceptional case. The last opportunity finally came at the 1984 Boston Marathon. It was the last official race on the last day of the qualifying period to obtain a qualifying mark.

HIGH DRAMA ON PATRIOTS' DAY

I had spent the last 10 years advocating for women's distance races to be included in the Olympic Games, and now I was president of the International Runners Committee, lobbying for adding women's 5000- and 10,000-meter races as well as the marathon into the Olympic program. With the marathon in the Games, it was more important than anything in the world to me to qualify for those Trials.

After the marathon was approved, the 5000 and 10,000 were orphaned events. Our federation did not support us so we, the IRC, brought an international class-action lawsuit against the IOC and all the entities working under them. The relevant fact here is that our case was coming to court for the first time, in Los Angeles, the same April day when I had to be in Boston. The ACLU represented us, and lead lawyer

143

Susan McGrievy went to court as I went to the marathon starting line.

Two separate news crews were following me around Boston that day. They had me wear a microphone until the start, when I declared my quiet time before going to the line. Also I had to tell them no, I would not stop at the halfway mark to talk.

The ABC news crew focused on the story line, "Former Boston winner returns. Will she win?" I could have told them, 11 years later, that was just not going to happen. The other crew was focused on the lawsuit in court that day. No stress, right? Did I mention drama?

Another complication actually made me cry. My roommate for that trip was a woman runner from Florida, Sharon Chiong, so we two warm-climate runners stood at our window the morning of the race, watching the rain and hail blow against our window in a chill. She said we had nothing to lose and we had to try. I knew she was right. We were not alone in our quest for qualifying times.

All these women were particularly bonded that day and tried to run together in mutual support. We shared extra clothing and tried to dress as warmly but efficiently as we could. Even with tights and long sleeves, the rain and hail felt like little arrows flying into my skin. The first thing I remember about the splits en route was the fact that they made sense.

In my previous races in Boston, I heard splits as I entered each new town, with odd distances given in fractions of a mile that no one could calculate. This time, I knew every five miles that I was on pace, all the way to 25 miles, where I saw a digital timer telling me that I was in 10th place and my projected finish time was 2:44. The last thing I remember was wondering how they did that. Maybe I was hallucinating.

(Dave McGillivray, the current Boston race director, verified that clocks that project finish time have been used for some time for the leaders of the race. So yes, I did really see it, and this was not an hallucination.)

At that point, I began to feel like I was fighting against falling forward face first, and I started to get tunnel vision. My reaction? I got mad and yelled to myself, "It's one more mile! I deserve to finish!" And I began to chant to myself: "I *deserve* to finish."

When I woke up on the hospital cot with an IV bottle hanging overhead and dog tags around my neck, in a woolen blanket, the doctor said, "We're keeping you here for observation. Your temperature is below 93-degrees." I responded with teeth chattering out of control, "Did I finish? What was my time?" He made a joke to the nurse that, although I was dying, I'd like to know my time. She went away to find out. My watch was still running, so I did not know and *had* to know.

While we waited, the doctor asked where my bag and dry clothes were. I said that I had expected to jog back to my hotel from the finish, so did not send clothes here. When the nurse returned, she said I had finished in 14th place with 2:47-plus. I rounded up to 2:48 and figured that according to the last clock I saw, I had lost four minutes and four places in one mile. Oh my, I must have looked like I was running in place. But I made it! I was qualified! I was a sick puppy but a happy one.

The news crews were all over themselves looking for footage of "the fall" at the finish line, but to my good fortune they did not find any. However, my husband said I was on "Nightline" that night, looking like a drowned rat. Nice. I said, "Book those tickets to Olympia [Washington] for the Trials."

145

Then I got a message from Julie Cart of the *Los Angeles Times*. We had lost our case in court that same day. I went from such a high point to the lowest in minutes. I call this the most dramatic day in my entire running career.

Qualifying for the Olympic Trials at the 1984 Boston Marathon.

24. Our Trials

Change is the law of life
And those who look only
To the past or present
Are certain to miss the future.

John F. Kennedy

"Finally." That's what the Nike ad said on the back of the program for the first U.S. Women's Olympic Trials Marathon, held in Olympia, Washington. Finally women are included on the Olympic schedule. Finally hundreds of distance runners have a new goal to strive for. And finally the day for U.S. team selection had arrived.

It was a greatly anticipated moment, finally to walk to the starting line with more than 200 other women runners. For some, this race had served as motivation to reach a tangible goal – at the least, a 2:51:16 qualifying time. For some, it was the best – not necessarily the only – choice left open for a chance at Olympic participation, for lack of other distances (5000 or 10,000 meters) to run.

For only three women, it could be the realization of an Olympic dream. For all, it was a momentous occasion. Scarcely a person in Olympia had not contributed in at least a small way to the day's festivities, if only to turn out and cheer. And cheer they did.

147

The 56 seeded runners took their assigned positions on the starting line, and the rest of us positioned ourselves at random behind them. There was lots of well-wishing among the women, everyone hoping for PRs. Nearly everyone readied watches for the countdown to the start. A notable exception was Julie Brown, who wore no watch at all. She and a few others were obviously more concerned with place than pace.

Out for a PR myself, I didn't dare look up for the balloons or whatever signaled the start. It was not the time to celebrate yet, just time to race. Until things steadied a little after the first mile or two, I knew I'd have to be alert to run in the thick pack. Lots of hands went up, steadying runners against tripping and crowding. No one seemed to rabbit out front. All seemed content to stay together at a reasonable pace.

I was trying to anticipate a good performance in the most optimistic terms possible. In reality, the Boston race was still in my legs, and my already fragile immune system was severely compromised from that ordeal. A positive attitude cannot make up for a less than fully prepared physical body.

While I may have thought I'd be running in a race in which I knew everyone, the truth was that I could not put many names with faces. Yet it was pleasant to recognize some "faces from the past," like Kim Merritt, Judy Gumbs-Leydig and Katy Schilly. As Kim and I ran along together, she became upset when she registered a 6:10 mile split. (Sub-2:40s were not in the stars for either of us that day, but she managed a respectable 2:43.) Maybe it occurred to Kim, as it did to me, that had we been given this opportunity, say, prior to the Montreal Games, we might have been Olympic teammates.

My pace seemed to hold steady until about the halfway mark. I knew there were more hills in the first half than in the last, so I took heart from my early splits. I tried to concentrate on getting from one aid station to the next or from one-mile marker to the next. The stations were perfect. No one had ever before handed me cups of water with caps and straws. Certainly I had never been given sponges shaped like pineapples (thanks to a sponsor, Dole).

In addition to the provided electrolyte drink, we were allowed personal "specialized fluids." My own ERG awaited me every five kilometers at the same location on the middle table. I could count on it. If all else failed, a backup table provided water for those who missed the first round.

In spite of best-laid plans, my pace went awry. While I'd like to say that I dropped back in the pack to experience the whole spectrum of the race, the plain truth was that the choice wasn't mine to make. I could easily have joined the 40 or so dropouts, but I chose to experience the finish the only way I could and still salvage my screaming hamstrings: slowly.

I should not have been surprised that my body betrayed me. It was less than four weeks since my qualifying race at Boston, where I had blacked out from hypothermia, and this was my fourth marathon in as many months. I resigned myself to just finishing.

For the first time, I looked around at the beautiful scenery. There was one street, completely canopied by lush green foliage overhead. There was Capitol Dome looming over Capitol Lake, and green-forested hills all around. The streets were lined with thousands of cheering supporters.

In addition to the crowd enthusiasm, I was touched by the support of my fellow competitors. As my own

149

race soured, I often slowed to walk and took comfort in stretching out painful muscles at the aid stations. Seemingly every runner who passed by me offered a kind word. The camaraderie was wonderful. We were bonded in an historic moment.

We were applauded for the entire last mile (it was dubbed the "Miracle Mile"). No matter our place or pace, the cheering fans reminded us more than ever what a special moment this was for each of us. After the race, in the finish area, the Olympian treatment continued as we were bedecked with flower leis, treated by medical crews and massage therapists, and supplied with food and drink. Our every need was met.

Later a dear friend, trying to salve my disappointment, offered consolation that I wish I could share with those who had not been able to finish and others, like me, who were disappointed with their finish. We had come to run like the champions we are, she said. No one could fault those of us who tried to run better than we ever had. It reminded me of something I said before my qualifying performance at Boston the month before: "There's no shame in trying and failing, only in not trying at all."

This was the day to celebrate our first-ever U.S. Olympic women's marathon team. Joan Benoit was the victor. As Amby Burfoot aptly stated in *Runner's World's* coverage of this race: "No matter from what angle we survey Benoit's Trials victory in 2:31:04 on May 12, no matter how dispassionately we attempt to measure her achievement or how many other marathon performances we hold it up against, the same ineluctable conclusion presents itself: this was the greatest individual marathon effort of all time."

Joan had endured a lot in the weeks leading up to the most important race of her life. This included knee surgery 17 days earlier, and as if that were not enough, her hamstring muscles tightened up in reaction to the surgery, leaving her with two potential time bombs that could sideline her at any moment. She prevailed and in world-class style. Her new teammates joining that historic team were Julie Brown (2:31:41) and Julie Isphording (2:32:26), who declared, upon finishing, that dreams do come true.

Women's marathon pioneers at a pre-Trials event in Olympia, Washington, 1983. Honorees included Nina Kuscsik, Bobbi Gibb, Doris Brown Heritage, Beth Bonner, Cheryl Flanagan (Bridges Treworgy), Judy Ikenberry, Sharon Barbano, Miki Gorman.

25. Golden Day in L.A.

Your living is determined not so much by what life brings to you as by the attitude you bring to life; not so much by what happens to you as by the way your mind looks at what happens.

Kahlil Gibran

Between the Marathon Trials and the Olympic Games, I was honored by the ACLU at an awards ceremony celebrating "Champions of Justice" at the ACLU's 25th Annual Garden Party, at the home of Betty and Stanley Sheinbaum. Tributes were paid to "stars in their respective athletic fields as well as individuals who have furthered the cause of civil liberties," said Ramona Ripston, ACLU executive director. "Their experiences on and off the playing field have led to advancing equality through the examples they have set and the challenges to fundamental rights they have faced." Athletes honored included Rafer Johnson, Harry Edwards, John Carlos and Mac Robinson. Mayor Tom Bradley was our "special guest speaker."

I loved that my friend Sherrill Kushner, a lawyer, placed an ad in the program for the event quoting Pierre de Coubertin, who said in 1912, "We feel that the Olympics must be reserved for men… and female applause as reward." Sherrill's response: "Eat your heart out, Pierre!"

Had the International Runners Committee/American Civil Liberties Union lawsuit for the women's 5000 and

10,000 been successful and led to inclusion of these events in the 1984 Olympic Games, the makeup and perhaps the outcome of not only the U.S. Olympic Trials Marathon might have changed entirely, but also perhaps the selection of women's Olympic Marathon teams would have been affected worldwide.

Many women, including myself, were deeply disappointed by the absence of the 5000 and 10,000 in the Olympic Games. Certainly the significance of the marathon's inclusion should not be overlooked. But it was ironic that, in a year when there was a distance as long as the marathon, there were no other options for women distance runners.

Lorraine Moller won the 1984 Boston Marathon to ensure a spot on the New Zealand Olympic Marathon team. But her friend and countrywoman Allison Roe, unable to finish Boston, would not be going to Los Angeles. Several other world-class runners would not find a spot on the New Zealand team, either. As Moller put it, "There are not enough races to go around."

I was delighted to host Joan Benoit in Santa Monica for the duration of her Los Angeles stay. Sherrill Kushner lived in my neighborhood and generously offered up her guesthouse for Joan's privacy and solitude in preparation for her race. At the time, Tom, Michael and I were living in an apartment in Santa Monica rather than Topanga.

My place offered just two bedrooms in a small space on a busy street, with a four-year-old child and a night owl for a husband. Joanie was better off at Sherrill's more spacious home, several blocks away, with accessibility to the favorable running routes on San Vicente Boulevard and Santa Monica beaches.

In fact, Tom and I had lots of friends who willingly offered their homes in Santa Monica to visiting

Olympians. Especially our marathoner friends were grateful to be housed away from University of Southern California athletes' housing for far better training sites near the beach. I remember Australian Rob De Castella bringing an entire entourage along with him, including his family and a massage therapist.

On the day I settled Joanie in Sherrill's house, I kept an appointment with my long-time friend and everyone's favorite foot doctor, John Pagliano. I was nursing another stress fracture. U.S. Olympic marathoner Julie Isphording went along with me, I suppose for a second opinion about her own ailments. This was not a good sign. (Sadly, the injury would not allow Julie to finish the Olympic race.)

In the days surrounding the Games, I spent a lot of time pool-running and participating in so many aqua aerobics classes that Lynda Huey, creator of "Water Power Workout," made me her first instructor (which I continued to teach for decades afterward). As well, I was still plagued with chronic sinusitis, and was undergoing allergy tests and shots in an attempt to return to normalcy now that we had returned to Los Angeles for good, to my great relief. Then there were Olympic Committee meetings and trainings for volunteers and employees.

Both Tom and I played roles in the L.A. Olympic Organizing Committee. Tom was the co-director, with John Brennand, of the men's and women's marathons. I had only a minor part in the staging of the race – a volunteer role that kept me close to the women runners at all times, but out of the public eye and off any list of names in print.

I was certainly blacklisted by the LAOOC for bringing the lawsuit. One day, I got on an elevator in the LAOOC building where Tom worked, and H.D.

154

Thoreau, head of the Olympic track and field program for 1984, spoke disparagingly of me to his colleague in a whisper loud enough for me to hear. Yes, I was blacklisted and knew it.

In fact, once the president of the LAOOC, Peter Ueberroth, discovered that Tom was my husband, he fired Tom. At least he tried. The marathon race committee, under co-director John Brennand's lead, refused to move forward without Tom and they prevailed (unbeknownst to Ueberroth).

As a volunteer, I was able to view nearly all of the track and field events at the Coliseum. We chose to attend the final dress rehearsal of the opening ceremonies, for the highlights without all the crowds and traffic.

The day before the women's marathon, I delivered Joan Benoit's and Julie Brown's water bottles for placement along the course, obtained maps of the course (for their friends and family) and picked up tickets for the start at Santa Monica College. I recorded in my running log, "Is this really the Olympic Women's Marathon?!" I was elated to be there, in any capacity. Here is what I wrote afterward:

First Women's Olympic Marathon. My day began early as a volunteer on the "Start Committee." It was arranged that Sherrill would deliver Joanie and that Glen would deliver Michael at the start of the women's race. We'd leave for the Coliseum after, or should I say the rest of us would follow Joan? Glen and Sherrill had tickets, thanks to Joan, and Michael and I got ours weeks ago.

Once at the Coliseum, my usher was a woman runner/friend, so we shared better seats available trackside for the spectacular finish. Michael was frightened at the hysteria that broke out in the crowd at

155

Joan's entrance – which I explained to Michael was "happy crying." But ultimately he was proud of "his friend Joanie." What an inspiration she was that day! From the finish line, through dinner at The Chronicle restaurant in Santa Monica, she never stopped smiling.

Her/my dream come true had a joyous ending shared by both of us. As I watched this dream unfold that day, it occurred to me that young girls all over the world were watching Joan Benoit on television, winning the Olympic Marathon, knowing they too could grow up to be Olympic champions if they wanted. They could dream of being presidential candidates and astronauts, too. It was an exciting time to be a woman.

With Michael and Joan Benoit (Samuelson) after her Olympic Marathon victory, at the home of Sherrill Kushner in Santa Monica, California.

156

26. Journey Continues

On coming full circle:
This day I breathed first-time is come round,
And where I did begin, there shall I end.
My life is run his compass.

Shakespeare

Approaching 40 years of age, my running was coming full circle. The mile (or metric mile) was what I first trained to run, and remained my favorite event. Now I was returning to the middle distances, 1500 to 5000 meters, and becoming a masters athlete meant I had a new ballpark to play in.

In 1987, I participated in a number of masters track meets and set my goals on the upcoming World Veterans Track and Field Championships in Melbourne, Australia, that December. The first step in the complicated journey to Melbourne included my assignment as the head U.S. team coach for an international championship 15-kilometer road race held in Monaco in November. Not wanting to give up either trip, I made travel plans to get from one to the other and plotted my training accordingly.

At least traveling with some of the top U.S. women for the first half of my journey afforded me some remarkable training partners and ensured that workouts would happen every day. The women on the team celebrated my November birthday with me in Monaco, and together we celebrated their team win at the championship race. It was an amazing time!

The hard part was flying from Europe to Los Angeles, stopping overnight at home, gathering my family and my pre-packed baggage, then heading back to the airport for the trip to Australia via Hawaii. My strategy? Sleep whenever possible. Sleep on the plane, sleep in the hotel; just sleep anywhere I sat still. Upon arrival in Melbourne, I slept the better part of a day and a half, completely missing my pre-race tune-up workout day. It worked.

The first event was the 1500 meters, and it was run in terribly dry, hot and windy conditions. I had a perfectly executed race plan, and I won. The part I remember the most was the joy of the victory lap, feeling so exalted that I laughed the entire way around the oval, thinking how much easier four laps could feel compared to a marathon. Welcome back to middle distances!

That joy turned to despair when I awoke the next morning with an allergy attack from the dry and dusty winds. I had a severe sore throat, and knew I was falling ill. The weather had also taken a turn for the worse. As it was explained to me, those dry, hot winds traveled across the plains, headed down around the South Pole, and returned with hail, rain and freezing winds. This only worsened my condition.

As I watched the rain and hail beating against my hotel windowpane, Tom and I learned that many of the track and field events were being cancelled due to the high winds and the downpour. That is, events were cancelled except for the distance races. They were always run, no matter what.

I was examined by a doctor who determined that there was no danger in my running, that I might not

158

perform up to expectations but that I was going to suffer my symptoms for the rest of the week with or without running. Since I would not travel this far for just one race, I went ahead with the 5000. It reminded me of the Boston Marathon in 1984. Once again, I prevailed.

Perhaps my poor state of health forced me to start conservatively. When I reached the mid-point of the race, I noticed that I wasn't breathing any harder than anyone else in the race and I made a surge. No one went with me, so I kept picking up the pace.

Running 5000 meters translates into 12½ laps around the track, and every runner here was assigned to a personal lap-counter to keep things organized. Mine was a young girl. When I made that move to take the lead, she jumped up from her chair on the infield, and the wind blew it away. That's how strong the winds were.

Also it was odd to see that the only spectators were inside the press box and no one was outside in the stands. I could see them clapping but could not hear them. When I crossed the finish line in first, a kind official bundled me up in a wool blanket and whisked me inside. I spent the rest of the week sick in bed, sipping hot tea and enjoying my two gold medals.

In a symbolic gesture, I dedicated my 1500-meter race to Laszlo Tabori and presented him with my medal. It was in memory of his race in the 1956 Olympics in Melbourne, the last time he represented his home country of Hungary before defecting to the United States after the Hungarian Revolution. He missed his chance for an Olympic medal by a split second, no doubt due to the underlying conditions. I thought of him with gratitude for the running career he made possible for me.

That same year, 1987, was when my coaching career began. I was already assigned as the U.S. women's head coach on trips to Monaco, Taiwan and Japan (several times). But while this was an honor, the position was more as a figurehead than the runners' actual coach. However, I became a hands-on, daily track coach/P.E. teacher of all the kids in my son's elementary school. I learned that if you can convince kindergartners to run, jump and throw, or even just pay attention, you've acquired the basic skills to coach just about everyone else.

In 1988, the year the women's 10,000 was added to the Olympic Games in Seoul, I went on to work at the LA84 Foundation (formerly the Amateur Athletic Foundation). Through 1991, I designed and directed a distance running program for middle-school children throughout Los Angeles County, while also coaching the program at my son's middle school. From there I coached at two high schools, and became an athletic director, health and physical education teacher.

I made one more attempt at a World Veterans title, but fell short with a knee injury in 1991, had surgery and never quite recovered. At that point I retired from running and took up swimming.

As a family, we thoroughly enjoyed attending the Barcelona Olympics in 1992. Tom was working for Reebok, with Pat Devaney and Joe Vigil. They put our 12-year-old Michael to work outfitting athletes with shoes and apparel. He came home with an amazing collection of pins and autographs, meeting famous athletes in all sports, not just track and field. In fact, we enjoyed a lot of meets on the international circuit as Tom worked as an agent for many track and field athletes overseas.

In 1996, I came out of running retirement to participate in the 100th Boston Marathon, after which I combined pool running and land running to extend my recreational running life a few more years. I also coached Team Diabetes from the mid-1990s through the early 2000s. But after the tragic events of September 11th, 2001, there was a marked decline in traveling and fund-raising efforts in the charity world and beyond, which caused the team to dissolve.

By then, I was assisting with coaching a local women's team, and I continued coaching high school track and cross-country teams – as I do still today. While earning my Masters degree in Education and teaching credential in Health Education at Loyola Marymount University in 2000, I moved from high school coaching back to LA84 to become Director of Coaching Education. In 2004, I received a Lifetime Achievement Award from Southern California USA Track and Field.

My best friend in life, Jeaney Garcia, presented me for that award with a tribute worthy of a queen. Eleanor Roosevelt once said: "Many people will walk in and out of your life, but only true friends will leave footprints on your heart." Jeaney continues to model the most positive influence on me.

Over the years, my surgery count reached 14, with only 13 comebacks. I now spend my daily workout time mostly walking or pool-running at Loyola Marymount, where I am currently working in the School of Education. I teach Health Education online courses to teaching credential candidates. I also speak at coaching workshops for the LA84 Foundation. In other words, I teach teachers and coach coaches.

In 2012, I was inducted into the National Distance Running Hall of Fame. Preparation for my acceptance speech was a different experience from previous inductions to other halls – no more or less prestigious, but unique in that I could share this one with a much broader audience thanks to having so many social networks at our fingertips.

Lately, life has been full of joyous reunions and reconnecting with many friends. It has also been a good time for reflecting on my running career. I've been gathering stories and photos on my website (www.jacquelinehansen.com), writing articles and making appearances to speak on the history of women's running.

One friend, Ike Carpenter, who remembers Tom as not just his boss but also a father figure, made a comment to me that really tugged at my heartstrings. He said, "There are two kinds of runners, those who run to escape their demons and those who run to celebrate their role in this thing called life. You have always struck me as the latter."

Tom used to say that I "sang" when I ran. I suppose I was happiest when running. As I reflect back, I am grateful for the life experiences and opportunities I've enjoyed, in great part due to running. I've enjoyed the journey of living women's running history.

The Boston Marathon continues to play an integral role in my life. On April 15, 2013, I was honored for my 40th anniversary of winning Boston at the "Champion's Breakfast," and by being the official race starter of the elite women's race. My strongest advocate on the BAA Board is the kind and capable Gloria Ratti, vice president. She provides truly royal treatment for honored guests. I made appearances at events several times a day every day, and the atmosphere was joyous and celebratory.

To add to the celebration, three of the athletes whom I coach purposefully qualified for this particular Boston in order to join me for the occasion. Once I started the race, I was brought to the finish line via a police escort, in time to watch the leaders of both the men's and women's races. I was seated in the VIP grandstands overlooking the finish line.

Not content to stay put, I made my way to the street level to greet each of my runners when they crossed the finish line, escorting them through the finish chutes, then across Copley Square to the hotel.

It was upon my third round-trip that I delayed because, according to the updates sent to my cell phone on each runner's time splits, the third one, Jeaney Garcia, was falling behind pace. So I waited for my first runner, Charlie Gardner, to finish showering, leaving the second runner, Deborah Hafford, to bathe before going back for Jeaney.

From the hotel lobby, Charlie and I felt and heard two explosions, like an earthquake and sonic boom together. I wanted so much to believe it was an accident, like a gas leak in a construction site we could see nearby. But when we stepped off the curb, we were stopped by dozens of emergency vehicles, sirens screaming, flying by us and heading straight for the finish line.

We were turned back from the finish area by race committee personnel, and we really only went inside my hotel to use land-line phones and the Internet since all cell phone usage was cut off immediately. There we were retained on lockdown for the remainder of the day and evening. It was seemingly hours before we reunited with Jeaney, who was diverted off course less than a mile from the finish.

It was a tragedy beyond my comprehension, one that haunts me still. Upon returning home I attended all memorial runs that came to my attention. I felt a need to connect with people doing something positive in the wake of the harrowing tragedy. As a kind and wise colleague at work, Maureen Herbert, once suggested to me, I decided to take her advice and train to walk the whole marathon in 2014. I will return to Boston, of that I am certain. My Associate Dean at LMU, Kathy Ash, has offered to do this with me. We are counting the days, and we are far from alone.

My stories portray my life as that child of the sixties, who became a feminist in the seventies and a soccer mom in the eighties. I suppose I spent a good deal of the nineties, and beyond, on giving back to the sport that gave me such rich life experiences. Looking back, I would do it all over again in a heartbeat.

With Jeaney Garcia and basketball coaching legend John Wooden.

Author's Note

Sooner or later we all discover that the important moments in life are not the advertised ones, not the birthdays, the graduations, the weddings, not the great goals achieved. The real milestones are less prepossessing. They come to the door of memory unannounced, stray dogs that amble in, sniff around a bit and simply never leave. Our lives are measured by these.

Susan B. Anthony

I retired from what is known as "open" competition in 1984 and later joined "masters" racing (35 years-plus) until 1992, when knee surgery was not successful. I turned to masters swim teams for workouts instead, but first I needed to learn to swim. I loved the similarity to track training with the intervals practiced and endorphins provided! I even qualified for my lifeguard certificate and taught aqua-aerobics. However, after rotator cuff surgery (total of three), I no longer swim. Now I just pool run, and walk and hike.

This process of retiring, combined with pure and simple aging, led me to reflect a lot about my life. Funny how the older I get, and the more removed from the daily activity of running, the wiser and more knowledgeable I seem. I have a newfound perspective, and while I've been called a "visionary," I love seeing the whole picture, the connections, or the "circle game." As Joni Mitchell sings, "We're captive on the carousel of time, we can't return, we can only look behind from where we came, and go 'round and 'round in the circle game."

I am grateful to, oh, so many supportive people I am fortunate to hold close around me. Thanks to Joe Henderson for providing the map and directions for this book. He believed in my project, much the same way he believed in our founding of the International Runners Committee (IRC). Joe kept us on track toward our mission for women's rights to run, while he chronicled the years of progress in our newsletters as well.

Janet Heinonen took over publishing the IRC newsletter, and has always been my friend, was my support team at my PR marathon in Eugene, and is now co-authoring our book on the history of women's running. Her husband Tom Heinonen coached me through the 1984 Olympic Trials, when I moved to Oregon in those years.

Leal-Ann Reinhart, my best friend, ran and traveled with me during the peak years with Laszlo Tabori. She became a national marathon champion in 1977, when I got to cheer her along the course. We continue to share a deep friendship, and her influence permeates my life story.

I went with Leal-Ann to the National Women's Conference in 1977, broadening my horizons about women's rights. To this day, my favorite quotation comes from Jill Ruckelshaus' speech that year at the California Convention of the National Women's Political Caucus. She concluded with "… at the end of your days, you will be able to look back and say that once in your life, you gave everything you had for justice."

Thanks to Leal-Ann, Janet and Joe (the real writers) for your combined efforts toward our cause.

When I met Fran Vella at the 2013 Napa Valley Marathon, she informed me that she did proof-reading as a profession and offered to help with the book if needed. How could she know "fresh eyes" were exactly what I needed? It was fortuitous, and I am so grateful for her expertise. It is comforting to know that editing and proofing were both in the hands of professionals, who were also expert in running. I am so fortunate.

From the time I thought about running a marathon, then thought about running an ultra-marathon, and later when writing a book was just a brainstorm, I have appreciated encouragement from Patrick Miller and Jim Pearson. Patrick's perspective and experience as a runner and author helped me verbalize concepts I struggled to define. From the beginning of my career, it was his suggestion that I go to Boston and, as they say, the rest is history.

Jim has run a mile in my shoes – 50 of them, to be exact. A national champion at 50 miles, he competed in the 1978 race when I ran that distance. He has since encouraged me to tell my stories, and as an English teacher and coach he earned the right to pester me until this book's completion.

Guiding me across the digital divide was Linda Wallace. I am indebted to her for going above and beyond friendship and support to creating my website (jacquelinehansen.com) and joining every conceivable social network. She reformed herself from being an athlete, teacher and coach like me, into becoming a technology director. I learn constantly from her. We support one another on a daily basis.

Thank you to Wayne Wilson, Shirley Ito and Michael Salmon for help with endless research needs at the LA84 Library – as well as all their supportive endeavors toward one of my favorite roles, as director of the LA84 Foundation Coaching Education Program.

Thank you to Patrick Escobar and Anita DeFrantz for bringing me into the LA84 Foundation family. I'm very grateful that Anita introduced me to Peter Jerome, to work on the women ski jumpers' lawsuit, which paralleled the women runners' case.

A lot of gratitude goes to Ramona Ripston and Susan McGrievy and the Southern California Chapter of the ACLU for representing us in our lawsuit. Thanks go to Nike for funding and founding the International Runners Committee, with thanks to the members of the committee and the more than 70 women from nearly 30 countries who signed right-to sue letters to bring the lawsuit.

My work toward equality in running has been a shared quest. To that end, this book is a tribute to everyone who helped to make it possible. This story is *ours*, not just mine.

Women's distance races were a long time coming, whether you count back from the ancient or modern Olympic Games – or at least to 1928, when the 800-meter race was "given" to us and then "taken back" after those Games. This book also has been a long time coming. I've been writing blogs as first drafts for a few years now, in anticipation of a book, and I've been writing journals for more than 40 years. Possible books have been rattling around in my head most of my running life. Now, at last, this book has a life of its own.

Appendices:
Stories and Statistics

Our Marathon Movement

This is a more general history of the event, which I wrote for the January/February 2012 issue of Marathon & Beyond *magazine. Thanks to publisher Jan Seeley and editor Rich Benyo for allowing me to reprint the article here. Some segments are covered in greater or lesser detail elsewhere in this book.*

In 1896, a young woman by the name of Melpomene ran the men's Olympic marathon course during the Olympic Games in Athens, Greece, but was not allowed to enter the Olympic stadium at the finish of her run. (There is a debate among sport historians whether another woman, Stamata Revithi, also did a similar feat or if she and Melpomene are the same person.) Women would need to wait for almost a century to run this distance officially at the Games, and the right to run *any* distance there was a long time coming.

A first step in that direction was an event that Alice Milliat created. This pioneer in women's sports, one of my heroines, organized the first Women's Olympic Games, which took place in Paris in 1922, after co-founding the Federation Sportive Feminine Internationale (FSFI) the year before. I am only disappointed that she did not continue on that path, but instead her efforts were co-opted by the International Olympic Committee (IOC), which demanded she not use the term "Olympic."

It is not surprising that women were treated in such

a manner. Soon after the modern Olympic Games were inaugurated, consider the speech by founder Pierre De Coubertin: "We feel that the Olympic Games must be reserved for men... the solemn and periodic exaltation of male athleticism with internationalism as a base, loyalty as a means, art for its setting and female applause as its reward."

Thus, in 1926, Milliat changed the name and held the "Women's World Games" in Gothenburg, Sweden. In return, women were given five events only in the 1928 Olympic Games, including the 800-meter race. The winner finished in world-record time, but because some of the women collapsed in exhaustion at the conclusion of that race, women were barred from running anything longer than 200 meters for the next 32 years. We know today that the event was misrepresented in international news reports. Seeing that the IOC severely restricted women's events and could revoke their events at any time, the FSFI continued to sponsor their own Women's World Games for a total of four up to 1934.

Subsequently, the IOC forced Milliat and the FSFI to hand over control of women's international athletics to the International Amateur Athletic Federation (IAAF), the governing body for track and field. The IAAF agreed to recognize women's world records and to extend the number of events on the Olympic program, not all of which came to fruition.

I only wish the Women's Olympic Games had continued. It took until 1960 to reinstate the women's 800-meter race. The fight for women's running events equal to men's would continue for decades to come.

From the outset, women distance runners had to forge their own way – not only with very little official support but, in fact, against a great deal of institutionalized resistance. Imagine the loneliness of the long-distance runner – especially female – back in 1918, when Marie Louise Ledru competed in a marathon in France. Or in 1926, when Violet Piercy of England clocked 3:40:22. And in 1951, when a "mystery woman in red" from Canada was reported to have competed in the Boston Marathon.

A milestone was reached in 1958 with the formation of the Road Runners Club of America (RRCA), a group that vowed to give women equal recognition. Not without reason have some of the largest women-only races emerged in New York City, home of the RRCA's founding.

In the 1960s, an attitude echoing that of the 1930s still prevailed, with this country's coaches concerned over the effect of running on a woman's "femininity" and her childbearing capabilities. Despite the unfavorable climate of opinion, a few women dared to be different. Lyn Carman and Merry Lepper had been training for and running in road races for some time when, in 1963, they jumped into the Western Hemisphere Marathon in Culver City, California. They sidestepped a race official who tried to stop them by declaring their right to public use of the roads. Lyn reportedly completed 20 miles of the race while Merry established a best marathon time of 3:37:07.

Also in 1963, Englishwoman Dale Greig began four minutes ahead of the field in the Isle of Wight Marathon. With an ambulance trailing her the entire route, she clocked 3:27:45, which has been claimed as the first recognized world marathon mark for women. Only two months later, that time was beaten by New Zealander Millie Sampson in the Owairaka Marathon with a 3:19:33. So much for running by women as mere play. The race was on! The women's marathon

172

movement had begun in earnest.

Back in the United States, the ever-famous – and traditionally all-male – Boston Marathon was infiltrated by one lone 23-year-old woman, Roberta Gibb, who in 1966 covered the distance in a reported unofficial time of 3:21. In 1967, she completed the Boston course in 3:27:17, a performance overshadowed by 4:20 finisher Kathrine Switzer's well-publicized encounter and ensuing battle with the race director, Jock Semple. In 1968, Gibb ran Boston in 3:40, and Marjorie Fish ran 4:45.

YOUNG WOMEN SET THE MARKS

Out of Canada in 1967 came an amazing report. A 15-year-old girl, Maureen Wilton, finished an otherwise all-male race in 3:15:23. Most of the world was astonished – indeed incredulous – with the possible exception of a doctor in the field of sports medicine and longtime advocate of women's distance running. From the small town of Waldniel in West Germany, Dr. Ernst Van Aaken had written, "What woman has not yet attained, she definitely will attain one day as the result of training methods specifically suited to her."

In his hometown, Van Aaken had trained such women as Marianne Weiss, Margaret Bach, Josefine Bongartz and Anni Pede-Erdkamp on consistent programs of 20 kilometers to 30 kilometers a day. Van Aaken, therefore, was little surprised at Maureen Wilton's performance. He backed his claim that any of his 800-meter runners could match it by arranging for a demonstration to satisfy the press a few weeks later. The result was yet another world best mark for Pede-Erdkamp in 3:07:26. This record stood until 1970, when in the United States 16-year-old Caroline Walker ran

3:02:53 in the Trail's End Marathon in Oregon.

Sara Mae Berman of Cambridge, Massachusetts, played a major role in the history of women's marathoning. She was the unofficial women's leader at the Boston Marathon in 1969, 1970 and 1971. Her 1970 time of 3:05:07 stood as an unofficial course record until 1974. As an official entrant, she finished fifth in both 1972 and 1973.

In 1969 at Boston, two other women finished: Elaine Pedersen and Nina Kuscsik. In 1970, a total of five women competed: Berman was followed by Kuscsik, Sandra Zerrangi, Diane Fournier and Switzer. The next year, 1971, saw only three finishers: Berman, Kuscsik and Switzer. But all those years of persistent effort and keeping their own times finally paid off.

In 1972, women were accepted for the first time as official entrants at Boston. Eight finished: Kuscsik won in 3:10:21, followed by Pedersen, Switzer, Pat Barrett, Berman, Valerie Rogosheske, Ginny Collins and Frances Morrison.

Honoring its founding pledge to promote distance running – male and female alike – the RRCA sponsored the American National Women's Marathon Championship in October 1970. The Amateur Athletic Union (AAU), which so far had not officially recognized women marathoners, did not sanction this closed club race in Atlantic City, New Jersey. Six women entered, and though they ran with men, all received equal consideration. That now-familiar runner, Sara Mae Berman, emerged the victor. Another milestone had been reached.

The world's fastest marathon improved three times in 1971 alone. Beth Bonner clocked 3:01:42 and then broke the three-hour mark for an historic first with 2:55:22 at the 1971 New York City Marathon, in close competition with Nina Kuscsik. That day they clocked the two fastest female times ever, with Nina doing 2:56:04.

At the 1971 AAU Convention, the Women's Committee increased the allowable competitive distance for women to 10 miles. Kuscsik commented: "The committee had come full circle and now approved what it had not previously allowed."

SERIOUSLY LOWERING MARATHON TIMES

By that year's end at the Western Hemisphere Marathon in Culver City, California, a technically illegal runner, Cheryl Bridges, slashed the women's best to 2:49:40 (the AAU had not yet recognized the marathon as an acceptable distance for women). Many witnesses to this feat were stunned that December day.

As Cheryl's Los Angeles Track Club teammate, I went to support her effort and was so engaged that I first considered running a marathon myself. Prior to that day, this would have been unimaginable for someone like me, who started as a fair-weather runner, only competing in track and only in the middle distances.

In 1972, the AAU recognized women as official entrants in marathons, although the Women's Committee insisted that the women start at a separate time or place. At the 1972 New York City Marathon, when chairwoman Pat Rico tried to enforce this rule, things came to a head.

Rico insisted that women start 10 minutes ahead of the men. The women participants took the position that since they were being scored and awarded prizes separately, theirs could be defined as a separate race without a head start. Ignoring the gun that fired for their

175

start, the women forfeited those precious 10 minutes before starting to run with the men. Nina Kuscsik, the first official women's winner at the Boston Marathon earlier that year, won the 1972 New York women's division in 3:18 – including the time penalty imposed for rebelliousness!

At the next AAU Convention, the Women's Committee resolved that women could start on the same line with men. This concession was more readily made in light of the report by Ken Foreman (Seattle coach and AAU official) that potential lawsuits were in the works over discriminatory practices at the Trail's End Marathon, where women were required to provide health certificates and men were not.

At Boston in 1973, I scored a victory in 3:05:59. A record number of 12 women started, and despite the high temperatures 10 finished.

Cheryl Bridges's marathon record finally fell in 1973 at the site where it was set, Culver City. Miki Gorman won the Western Hemisphere Marathon in 2:46:36. Gorman then set her sights on the Boston Marathon and won the 1974 women's division in a course record of 2:47:11.

The first AAU National Marathon Championships for women took place at San Mateo, California, in February 1974. Judy Ikenberry became the first officially recognized national champion with a time of 2:55:17. Forty-four of the 57 starters finished, with three runners under three hours. Eleven-year-old Mary Etta Boitano ran 3:01:13.

NorCal Running Review editor Jack Leydig wrote that the "overall [men's] winner, Jim Dare, was almost overlooked by the press as he became the fourth West Valley Marathon winner in as many years. Everyone was waiting for the winner of the women's nationals!"

Dr. Ernst Van Aaken, a strong advocate for women's running, hosted the first women's international marathon in his hometown of Waldniel, West Germany, in 1974. He had been arguing the case for women since the 1950s, when he fought for a German national championship in 800 meters in 1954. It took him 15 years more to implement the women's 1500 meters in the German federation program. In 1973, he held his country's first women's marathon.

FROM WALDNIEL TO CULVER CITY

I was not chosen for the U.S. team going to Waldniel for having missed the National AAU Marathon. However, a good friend and fellow distance runner, Bruce Dern, sponsored me to run in Germany. I placed fifth overall, breaking three hours in my third marathon, and came in first American, which the Germans tallied in the U.S. team points.

Ever grateful to Bruce for that opportunity, it gave me the confidence that I could compete with the world's best. I returned home to set my next goal at Culver City in December 1974. There I warmed up for the race with Bruce, who boasted about his ability to pick winners and at the same time calmed my nerves from all the talk about a possible assault on the women's record that day.

Miki Gorman's world best of 2:46:36 stood until late 1974, when Christa Vahlensiek and Chantal Langlace both completed marathons in faster times. Vahlensiek, however, was the victim of a short course. By the time certification was completed on Langlace's record of 2:46:24, I had bettered it with a 2:43:54 performance at the Western Hemisphere Marathon in Culver City – the third women's record to be set in that

177

race.

The record fell again at Boston in 1975. Van Aaken, present that day, had as much as predicted Liane Winter's 2:42:24. He said the record would not stand long. He predicted that his other protégée, Christa Vahlensiek, would run around 2:40 flat. In Germany, she scored a 2:40:15 the very next month.

Van Aaken further stated that, "If American [Jacqueline] Hansen found a favorable course, she would become the first woman to break 2:40." That October at the Nike-OTC Marathon in Eugene, Oregon, I ran 2:38:19 and set a world record as the first woman to run under 2:40. No wonder Van Aaken was called the "Wizard of Waldniel."

In 1976, Dr. van Aaken again hosted the Women's International Marathon in Waldniel, at his own expense. Nearly 60 women participated. Kim Merritt, that year's Boston winner (2:47:10), led to nearly 40 kilometers before succumbing to Vahlensiek, who decisively won in 2:45:24.

The 1976 AAU Championships were held in Culver City. Middle-distance ace Julie Brown, making her marathon debut, triumphed in 2:45:32. Teenager Diane Barrett finished less than 30 seconds behind, establishing a national junior record.

The year 1976 had begun with a historic precedent when the race organizers of Sao Silvestre, the New Year's Eve midnight run in Sao Paulo, Brazil, invited women to participate for the first time in its long, prestigious history. Vahlensiek and I finished first and second, respectively.

My invitation to Brazil evolved from a race in Puerto Rico six months prior. I had just won the San Juan 450 race when I met the race promoter from Brazil, who was recruiting international runners. I

178

eagerly volunteered, and he was most embarrassed to confess that there had never been a women's division in the Sao Silvestre. I encouraged him to create one and helped him to identify a potential women's field. He went home to convince his race committee, and perhaps in honor of the upcoming International Women's Year, it complied.

VALIANT EFFORTS AT 10,000

Back in the States, interest picked up at the 10-kilometer distance, most notably in the New York Mini-Marathon, where high school miler Julie Shea led the field of 500 women with a Central Park course record of 35:58. Little opportunity, however, was given to women to contest 10,000 meters on the track until a race held at Eugene, Oregon, in conjunction with the 1976 U.S. Olympic Marathon Trials. American women made clear to Olympic officialdom that they were perfectly capable of running long distances in competitive circumstances. Peg Neppel of Iowa State bettered the American record of Carol Cook (also of Iowa State) of 34:49.0 (1975) with 34:19.0, and Cook herself finished second in 34:42.2.

The increasing display of women marathoners racing worldwide apparently did not impress potentates from the International Amateur Athletics Federation (IAAF) and the International Olympic Committee (IOC). So political activists among women runners pursued other routes in an attempt to gain official recognition.

Showing the patience of Job, Nina Kuscsik and others tediously guided petitions and proposals through proper channels until, at long last, the AAU encouraged the USOC to present a proposal to the IOC that a

179

women's marathon be considered for inclusion in the 1980 Olympics. This proposal died in the wake of a similar modest proposal to include the 3000 meters, which was rejected. The committee argued the age-old myth of the inherent physical inability of women to withstand the rigors of racing more than two miles, let alone a whole marathon.

In 1977, the participation of women distance runners accelerated along with the evolving social phenomenon that became known as the "running boom." What was exciting was running with over 2000 women in the New York's Mini-Marathon that year. The marathon world record-holder, Chantal Langlace (2:35:15), took part and placed a strong third in the fast 10K.

Later in the year, Christa Vahlensiek regained her hold on the marathon mark with a 2:34:47. Kim Merritt broke my American record at Nike-OTC with a 2:37:57. And the number of women participating in the AAU Championships warranted a separate race, a neat production staged in Minneapolis. The new AAU marathon champion, Leal-Ann Reinhart, my teammate under the tutelage of Laszlo Tabori, ran 2:46:34.

The National Women's Conference was held in Houston in 1977 in recognition of the International Year of the Woman, in accordance with a United Nations declaration. The lofty goals of advancing women's contributions and removing sex barriers were enough to attract Leal-Ann Reinhart to attend the conference with me to seek help with our cause to advance women's distance running.

The magnitude and importance of the major issues considered by the conference delegates both empowered and humbled us to the point that we began to feel fortunate to be running at all and a little selfish about our quest. However, with the determination and tenacity of the marathoners that we were, we forged ahead. We were inspired by the presence of Bella Abzug, Gloria Steinem, Barbara Jordan, and Coretta Scott King. But it was the friendships of three women in particular that made a difference in our quest.

Peggy Kokernot was the young woman who played an integral role in the completion of a cross-country torch relay to open the conference. Her picture appeared on the cover of *Time* magazine and, in her words, her life changed in ways she could not have predicted. She introduced us to Mary Cullen of Houston, a runner and philanthropist whose support of the arts and athletics continues to this day.

Henley Gabeau (Gibble at the time) represented the RRCA in the coordination of the conference's torch relay. As she describes it, after meeting us in our lobbying effort for the inclusion of a women's marathon in the Olympic Games, she returned home with the mission for "the RRCA being a force in that effort." Jeff Darman, then the RRCA president, created a position for Henley as the chairwoman of the RRCA Women's Distance Committee. Both became members and tireless advocates of the International Runners Committee.

AVON STEPS UP

At the Avon International Marathon for women in 1978, 20 qualified women with sub-2:50 performances took part in a field of 186 runners from eight countries. The high temperatures of the day and the demands of the hilly course in Atlanta slowed the performance except for neophyte champion Marty Cooksey (2:46:16).

Second-place Sarolta Monspart (2:51:40) had more at stake than finishing in a good time. At home in Budapest, the Hungarian Athletic Federation had refused her permission to travel to Atlanta for the competition, so she secured it from the committee governing orienteering. Not only a world-class marathoner, Monspart was the 1972 world champion in orienteering. When her ruse was found out by the Athletics Federation, Monspart was told that she must place in the top five or never again be issued a visa to leave Hungary. She returned home inspired to organize women's marathoning there.

The 1978 Boston Marathon boasted 227 women participants in spite of the draw of the Avon marathon the month before. More than 4300 women took part in New York City's 10K Mini-Marathon. And the New York City Marathon was once again the site of the AAU Championships for women. By now, the race had left the confines of Central Park and had taken to the streets of New York, touching all five boroughs of the city.

In that race, the women's marathon movement took a great leap forward. Race announcer Toni Reavis, caught dumbfounded, relayed to an expectant crowd the number of the runner who was leading the women's race in apparent record time, but admitted that he was embarrassed at not being given her name. I scarcely knew the name. At least I did not associate it with marathoning.

She was among the best in the world at 1500 meters and more so at 3000 meters. But prior to the race, Manfred Steffny, the editor of Germany's prominent running publication *Spiridon* and Christa Vahlensiek's coach (and himself a former Olympic marathoner), told me that Vahlensiek had her eye on the Norwegian entrant. Grete Waitz was the International Cross-Country champion, and though her workouts hardly ever exceeded 10 miles, they were fast miles and often done twice a day.

Christa and I talked about this as we rode out to the starting line together that fateful day. When I was forced to drop out with a broken metatarsal bone in my foot, she found me at the same location with a similar injury of her own. We walked back to the finish line together to watch the outcome. Perhaps only Vahlensiek and Steffny were not surprised that October day when Grete Waitz clocked 2:30:30, breaking Christa's world record. What a crime that a marathon runner of such talent had no place in the upcoming Olympic Games solely because of her sex!

By 1978, activists in the movement were merging in mutual support. Going through channels had accomplished nothing, and begging for events was demeaning. By rights, the Olympic Games should have included a slate of women's distance events equal to that for men. That meant a 1500 meters (already one of the women's events), a 5000 meters, a 10,000 meters, a 3000-meter steeplechase and a marathon. Nothing less was fair or just – especially when top women runners, despite official obstructionism and meager competitive opportunities, had in the space of five years achieved times at these distances that most men had not matched in the first half-century of Olympic competition.

DEALING WITH THE OFFICIAL BODIES

On the other hand, women were put in the position of thanking the AAU (the governing body of track and field at the time, which became the Athletics Congress and eventually USA Track and Field, as it's known today) and the IAAF for their "support." At the same time, we were told to be patient, that progress takes time and that the IOC had good reason to hold back.

That "good reason" was defined in several parts, including the fact that not enough countries officially supported women's distance running. The IOC rulebook clearly noted the requirements for admitting new sports into the Olympics, but the standards for adding new events *within* an existing sport were vague. Rule 32 reads, "Only sports widely practiced by women in 25 countries and two continents may be included in the program of the Games of the Olympiad." Well, runners from that many nations participated in the 1979 International Marathon in Germany. Furthermore, how could any attentive observer of past Olympic Games accept this argument at face value?

Cursory research indicates that in the 1972 Games, for example, only eight countries entered teams in women's volleyball, six in men's field hockey, 16 each in water polo and team handball, and so forth, which reflected a lack of worldwide participation in these sports at the time. How many nations participated in whitewater canoeing at Munich? How many African and Arab countries, which at the time were often cast as the villainous objectors to women's distance running, supported the winter sports or yachting?

But more to the point, IAAF and IOC officialdom seemed to ignore or conveniently overlook the fact that until the 1960 Games, the marathon was more a sentimental, symbolic spectacle than a seriously contested and widely supported athletic event throughout the world. Until the 1932 Games, any nation could send an unlimited number of marathoners. In 1924 at Paris, seven Americans competed (and, after bronze medalist Clarence DeMar, none ran very well);

184

in 1928 at Amsterdam, 25 countries together sent a total of 79 entrants.

Limited to three entries each at the 1932 Los Angeles Olympics, only 18 nations were represented by a total of 32 runners. In 1948 at London, 30 of 41 marathoners from only 21 nations finished. The champion's time (2:34:52) was not quite as fast as the 1977 women's best of 2:34:47. At 44 years old, Miki Gorman would have placed ahead of the ninth man in London.

The persistent concern of the IOC about the physical capability of women to withstand the stress of endurance events was, by the mid-1970s, hardly worthy of rebuttal. The empirical data to the contrary compiled by such sports medicine researchers as Dr. Ernst Van Aaken, Dr. Barbara Drinkwater, Dr. Joan Ullyot and others from hundreds of competing women marathoners became overwhelming.

Of course, some of the IOC's continued reluctance to accept women's distance events might have been a political stance for dealing with the clamor from several other sports to be included in the Olympic program. But it would be foolish to regard this as the only factor.

WHY WAS THE IOC SO RELUCTANT?

The IOC appeared to have felt terribly threatened by the women's running movement. Perhaps beneath all of the organization's physiological and political arguments lay the cultural and psychological problems that, while less common today, have plagued the athletic establishment throughout history.

Looking at the overall picture from the perspective of more than 30 years later, it is hard to believe that resistance to expanding women's sports existed. It was

185

real, and it was due at best to apathy and at worst to discrimination. My outlook at the time was that "if you weren't part of the solution, then you were part of the problem." That was certainly true of people in power at every level in the governing bodies of our sport.

My favorite quote of the time was something that Dick Buerkle, a U.S. 5000-meter Olympian, said to me: "I cannot imagine what it must be like to fight for every event. I was born with the God-given right to run anything I want." His empathy was typical of the majority, if not all, of our male running colleagues.

In 1979, my husband, Tom Sturak, and I were founding members of an organization sponsored by Nike whose purpose was to increase competitive opportunities for runners worldwide and to help improve the administration of running. Our first objective was to seek a full program of women's distance races in the 1984 Olympic Games and in all other international championships leading up to the Los Angeles Games. The organization was named the International Runners Committee (IRC), and charter members besides myself and Tom Sturak included Joe Henderson, Eleanora Mendonca (Brazil), Joan Ullyot, Nina Kuscsik, Doris Brown Heritage, Jeff Darman, Leal-Ann Reinhart, Ken Young, Lynn Billington (England), Sarolta Monspart (Hungary), Henley Roughton (Gabeau), Manfred Steffny (West Germany), Arthur Lydiard (New Zealand), and Miki Gorman (Japan). When Joe Henderson stepped down from being the IRC newsletter editor, Janet Heinonen (Eugene, Oregon) joined as editor for the remainder of time the IRC was in existence.

By 1979, it was clear that things were changing. In that year, there were more international marathons for women than ever before. In Waldniel, 250 women from

25 nations met for a race that included outstanding performances of Joyce Smith and her victorious team from England. Smith, a 41-year-old mother of two daughters, was a lifelong runner with international titles at the middle distances. She ran the 1500 meters in 4:09.4 at the 1972 Games, she earned a bronze medal in the 3000 meters at the 1974 European Championships, and she was the International Cross-Country champion in 1972.

Smith competed in her first marathon in the 1979 British National Women's Championships, winning in 2:41:37. This earned her a trip to Waldniel later the same year, where she impressively took the title in 2:36:27, and 36 runners from 13 countries broke three hours. Smith long remained a world-class competitor, boasting a 2:29 PR earned when she was in her 40s.

Also in 1979, Twentieth Century-Fox staged an all-women's marathon with Tom Sturak as race director over the same Los Angeles course on which 1932 Olympic champion Juan Carlos Zabala ran 2:31:17. None of these women bettered Zabala's time, but they nonetheless proved they could go the distance. Beverly Shingles of New Zealand led the field of 56 to a victory in 2:56:46.

The same year, in the Tokyo Women's Marathon, 20 women from nine countries broke three hours. This was a production that only the Japanese could mount, fashioned after the elite, all-male marathon at Fukuoka. Again, Joyce Smith confirmed herself as a top-class marathoner, taking the title in 2:37:48.

FINALLY, SOME RECOGNITION

More significant than the good performances was the fact that the Tokyo race was the first women's-only marathon ever sanctioned by the IAAF. President Adriaan Paulen, who was present at Tokyo, declared his endorsement in this short speech (reprinted from IAAF Bulletin 28 and reprinted in the IRC Newsletter One):

"It is with a particular pleasure that I say these few words for this very special race, which brings to the Asian continent quite a new concept in women's athletics. Already in the USA and in Europe, the world's leading women marathon runners have gathered and surprised us all – not only by the vast number of finishers but also by the high quality of the leading performers, many of whom would finish high up in any men's marathon race.

"It would appear... in the realm of long-distance running that our lady athletes can come closest to the performances established by their male counterparts. The days are long since past when doctors and athletic leaders were worried about the medical advisability of women athletes competing. A rich fund of practical experience is now available for women long-distance runners... and there are also many good running publications which give wise advice.

"The athletes running today, by careful preparation and gradual buildup, are therefore ready for the challenge which this summit of distance races presents. Thanks to such races as the Waldniel [Marathon] in the Federal Republic of Germany in September and this inaugural race in Tokyo, the great impetus of women's long-distance running continues, and the movement will gather more and more support."

A positive turning point in the women's movement, this speech in Tokyo had been preceded (and influenced?) by Grete Waitz's historic performance in the 1979 New York City Marathon. Calling her 2:27:33 "the most advanced of women's achievements,"

Roberto Quercetani, European editor for *Track & Field News*, wrote in the December issue (as adapted for IRC Newsletter One):

"A time such as Grete's would have been good enough to earn a medal in an (all-male) Olympic Marathon as late as 1956. In terms of records, it was only in April 1935 that a male marathoner ran a bit faster than that. The Norwegian teacher thus appears to be 44 years behind the male clock. Before we regard this as a long lapse of time, let's consider the situation in other events. Women trail men by nearly 80 years at 100 meters and more than that at 400, 800 and 1500.

"It's in the distance events that the 'history gap' becomes decidedly narrower. Lyudmila Bragina showed the way in 1976 with her 8:27.2 3000, a mark first surpassed by a male running in 1926. That man, mind you, was Paavo Nurmi (whose best 1500-meter time has also been bettered by a woman, Olympic champion Tatyana Kazankina). Grete Waitz has gone further than any other woman athlete with her marathon record. That's why we referred to it as the most advanced of women's achievements in the sport."

A PREDICTION REALIZED

Four years after I clocked the first sub-2:40 marathon for women, my predictions for women's performances had come true. In 1975, I wanted other women runners to realize that my achievements were not so spectacular, that women would – indeed should – be running in the 2:20s within five years.

In March 1980, the IAAF decided that all international events with men's marathons would also have races for women and proposed that the IOC also consider adding the marathon to its agenda.

Unfortunately, when the IAAF asked the Los Angeles Olympic Organizing Committee for its support, the LAOOC replied that it was reluctant to accept the "burden" created by any expansion in the number of participating athletes.

"No sport is being singled out," the LAOOC wrote. "We are simply requesting all sports to assist us by resisting expansion. I trust you will understand." The IAAF did not understand but instead wondered why the Americans "had not put their house in order" on the issue.

In May 1980, the LAOOC still stood firm against adding any new women's events, but a women's marathon had gained written support from Los Angeles City Supervisor Kenneth Hahn. Another boost came from USOC member Bob Giegengack, who wrote in *New England Runner* that "track and field... is the number one Olympic sport. To tell us to run without women in a given event is like telling a baseball team to play without a second baseman because it costs too much." (The analogy seems to fit the 5000 and 10,000 meters even better.)

The USOC resolved to seek the LAOOC's unqualified support of the women's marathon. Incredibly and inexplicably, the IOC Program Commission (an Olympic consulting group responsible for sifting through the requests for new events) concluded just prior to the meeting at the Moscow Games, "We need more information. More medico-scientific research and experience need to be achieved."

Once again, it seemed that the women were out – and this at a time when demonstration sports like baseball were being considered seriously for inclusion. In Moscow, the IAAF took some firm steps forward. It recognized the 5000 and 10,000 meters as official world-record distances. It established that the 1983 IAAF World Championships in Helsinki would include a women's marathon. The 3000 meters and the 400-meter hurdles were added to the L.A. Olympic program as new women's events.

Telegrams flew back and forth from the International Runners Committee on the unresolved question of the Olympic marathon. Whether it was jeopardized by a backlash of officials angered over the U.S. boycott of the 1980 Moscow Olympics or because more important matters took precedence is unclear, but the women's marathon nearly became a dead issue. It was revived by the intervention of IAAF President Paulen and the now-enthusiastic support of the LAOOC.

Shortly before the Los Angeles meeting, confronted by the inexorable fact of another world record by Grete Waitz and a growing international clamor for justice, the IOC's general membership reversed the Program Commission's recommendation, opened the matter for reconsideration and delegated the authority to its nine-member Executive Board. In the last week of February 1981, almost a century after the idea was first proposed by a Greek runner, Melpomene, the Executive Board of the IOC made it official: the women's marathon would be added to the roster of Olympic events.

With Dr. Ernst Van Aaken (in wheelchair) at the first International Women's Marathon in Waldniel, West Germany. Those I can identify are (front row) Nina Kuscsik, Tom Sturak, me, Noel Tamini, Chantal Langlace, Judy Ikenberry. (back row) Van Aaken's nephew Jochen, Lucy Bunz, Marilyn Paul and Peggy Lyman. Kneeling beside Van Aaken is Ruth Anderson.

Life's Milestones

Many of the events listed below are described and discussed in detail with the chapters. Here is a just-the-facts listing for quick reference.

1948 – born in Binghamton, New York.

1957 – move to Los Angeles.

1966 – start running short races with Granada Hills High School's first girls' track and field team.

1967-69 – compete on track and field team at L.A. Pierce College.

1970 – start training with coach Laszlo Tabori.

1971 – join Los Angeles Track Club.

1972 – run and win first marathon, Western Hemisphere in Culver City, California.

1973 – win Boston Marathon... National Collegiate AIAW mile champion, representing Cal-State Northridge... win Charleston Distance Run of 15 miles... join Southern California Striders.

1974 – set American record for track six-mile (with 34:24)... place fifth (and first American) at International Women's Marathon Championships in Waldniel, West Germany... set world 15K road best in Florence, Italy (with 52:15)... break world marathon record as first sub-2:45 for women at Western Hemisphere, Culver City (with 2:43:54)... join Laszlo Tabori's own team, the San Fernando Valley Track Club.

1975 – set world marathon record again at Nike-OTC in Eugene, Oregon, with first sub-2:40 for women

(2:38:19)... win Honolulu Marathon with course record.

1975-76 – run first women's division at the Sao Silvestre, an historic New Year's Eve race in Sao Paulo, Brazil.

1976 – run women's exhibition 10,000 at Men's Olympic Marathon Trials in Eugene, Oregon. (Longest race for women at the Trials and Montreal Games was 1500 meters.)... run Women's International Marathon in Waldniel, West Germany.

1977 – marry Tom Sturak in Hawaii... attend National Women's Conference in Houston, Texas.

1978 – win National AAU 50-mile track title, setting 11 world records at intermediate distances... win Revco Marathon in Cleveland with course record.

1979 – win first of three titles (others in 1981 and 1982) at Catalina Marathon.

1980 – birth of son Michael.

1981 – move to Oregon.

1982 – win Oregon Track Club 30K with course and national age-group record.

1983 – move back to Los Angeles.

1984 – qualify at Boston for first U.S. Olympic Marathon Trials... run the first Trials at Olympia, Washington... volunteer at first Olympic race in Los Angeles... receive American Civil Liberties Union (ACLU) of Southern California Award for Leadership... inducted into Road Runners Club of America (RRCA) Hall of Fame... honored with The Athletics Congress-USA Annual Recognition Award as Woman of the Year.

1986-93 – "Water Power" Instructor with Lynda Huey's Athletic Network, Los Angeles.

1984-88 – Running Coach and Aqua Aerobics Instructor at International Sports Medicine Institute, Los Angeles.

1987 – win TAC-USA Masters Track and Field National Champion at 5000 meters (35-39 division)... win World Veterans Championships titles at 1500 and 5000 meters (for ages 35-39) in Melbourne, Australia.

1988 – inducted into Athletic Hall of Fame at California State University, Northridge.

1988-91 (fall semesters) – Amateur Athletic Foundation's Run for Fun Program Director, Los Angeles.

1988-93 (spring semesters) – track and field instructor at Topanga Elementary School.

1991-93 – Track and Field and Cross-Country Coach at Paul Revere Middle School, Los Angeles.

1994 – Assistant Track and Field Coach at Palisades High School, Pacific Palisades, California.

1994-2000 – Water Exercise Class Instructor at YMCA, Pacific Palisades.

1994-2000 – Athletic Director, Head Cross-Country and Track and Field Coach, Department Chair and Health and Physical Education Teacher at St. Monica Catholic High School, Santa Monica, California.

1997 – receive L.A. Pierce College "50 Distinguished Alumni" award in celebration of L.A. Pierce College's 50th anniversary.

1996 – run 100th Boston Marathon.

2000 – earn M.A. Degree in Secondary Education and Teaching Credential in Health Sciences from Loyola Marymount University.

2000-07 – Director of Coaching Education for LA84 Foundation of Los Angeles (formerly Amateur Athletic Foundation of L.A.).

2002-present – Health Education Instructor at Loyola Marymount University, School of Education.

2004 – receive Lifetime Achievement Award from Southern California Association-USATF.

2009-present – Business and Operations Coordinator for School of Education at Loyola Marymount University.

2011 – passing of husband Tom Sturak.

2012 – inducted into National Distance Running Hall of Fame.

2013 – honored at the Boston Marathon on 40th anniversary of winning there.

All My Marathons

Many thanks go to Ken Young for providing official statistics of the majority of my race results. What took me hours and days to comb through 40 years or more of journals, Ken could pull up in moments. I am so grateful to him!

There were many other "unofficial" marathons that I ran through. I didn't count them because they were simply for training, not competition.

1. Western Hemisphere at Culver City, CA (12/3/72) – 1st in 3:15:53.

2. Boston, MA (4/16/73) – 1st in 3:05:59, PR.

3. International Women's at Waldniel, West Germany (9/22/74) – 5th in 2:56:25, PR as 1st American.

4. Western Hemisphere at Culver City, CA (12/1/72) – 1st in 2:43:54, world record.

5. Nike-OTC at Eugene, OR (10/12/75) – 1st in 2:38:19, world record.

6. Honolulu, HI (12/14/75) – 1st in 2:49:24, course record.

7. Avenue of the Giants at Weott, CA (5/2/76) – 1st in 2:50:18.

8. International Women's at Waldniel, West Germany (10/2/76) – 8th in 2:55:50.

9. Western Hemisphere at Culver City, CA (12/4/77) – 1st in 2:50:33.

10. Revco at Cleveland, OH (5/14/78) – 1st in 2:46:59, course record.

11. AAU National 50-Mile at Santa Monica, CA (9/9/78) – marathon split of 3:11:50 (actually 26.7 miles), world track record along with 10 more at other intermediate distances.

12. Catalina Island, CA (3/25/79) – 1st in 3:26:51, course record.

13. Catalina Island, CA (3/22/81) – 1st in 3:23:40, course record.

14. Gales Creek Valley at Portland, OR (11/11/81) – 1st in 3:02:48.

15. Catalina Island, CA (3/21/82) – 1st in 3:26:19.

16. Nike-OTC at Eugene, OR (9/12/82) – 7th in 2:46:11.

17. Los Angeles International, CA (2/19/84) – 3:04 with walk/jog from 18 miles.

18. Los Alamitos, CA (3/10/84) – 2nd in 2:53:18.

19. Boston, MA (4/16/84) – 14th in 2:47:48, Olympic Trials qualifier.

20. U.S. Olympic Trials at Olympia, WA (5/12/84) – 3:00:28.

Races at Other Distances

I began competing with the Los Angeles Track Club in 1971 under Laszlo Tabori's coaching. We transitioned to the Southern California Striders in 1973, then in 1974 established our own San Fernando Valley Track Club. These results are a compilation from my running journals and in great part thanks again to statistician Ken Young's records. I have no record of short-distance races run during my earliest years in the sport.

1972:

Sunkist Indoor Meet at Los Angeles, CA (1/22/72) – mile in 5:13.

Westwood, CA (2/6/72) – 5th in mile, 5:10.

Oxnard, CA (2/13/72) – half-mile in 2:20, mile in 5:18.

International Cross-Country Qualifier at Seattle, WA (3/4/72) – 28th in 15:04 for 2.5 miles.

Valley College meet, CA (3/10/72) – half-mile in 2:18.

Mt. SAC Relays, CA (4/29/72) – 4th in 1500, 4:41.1.

Glendale College, CA (5/13/72) – 2nd in 1500, 4:41.

Cal-Poly Pomona, CA (5/21/72) – 1500 in 4:36, 2-mile relay in 9:14.

UC Irvine, CA (6/3/72) – 1st in 1500, 4:50.

Coliseum in Los Angeles, CA (6/4/72) – 1500 in 4:45.

Coliseum in Los Angeles, CA (6/9/72) – 1500 in 4:37.

State Meet at Hayward, CA (6/18/72) – 3rd in 1500, 4:40.

Track Nationals at Canton, OH (7/2/72) – 2nd in 2-mile relay, 9:13.

Ran cross-country season, but no results are now available.

1973:

Phoenix Invitational, AZ (3/25/73) – 2nd in 5000, 17:48.

Mt. SAC Relays, CA (4/28-29/73) – 1st in half-mile, 2:20.8; 1st in mile, 5:03; 1st in 2-mile, 10:45.

UCLA Collegiate Invitational, CA (5/4/73) – 1st in mile, 4:58.

AIAW Collegiate National Championships at Hayward, CA (5/11/73) – 1st in mile prelims, 5:03; (5/12/73) – 1st in mile final, 4:54.

Bay to Breakers at San Francisco, CA (5/20/73) – 2nd in 12K.

LaJolla track meet at San Diego, CA (5/28/73) – 1st in 2-mile, 10:47.

AAU State Championships at San Diego, CA (6/10/73) – 1st in 2-mile, 10:38.

Semana Nautica 15K at Santa Barbara, CA (7/4/73) – 1st in 1:01:15.

San Diego track meet, CA (7/7/73) – 1st in 5000, 17:26.2.

Santa Barbara, CA (1973) – 9 miles, 1246 yards in one-hour run.

Charleston Distance Run, WV (9/1/73) – 1st in 1:39:28 for 15 miles.

Blue Angels Cross-Country at Fountain Valley, CA (10/6/73) – 1st in 15:45 for race advertised as 5000 meters but likely less than 3 miles.

Centinela Park Cross-Country at Inglewood, CA (11/10/73) – 1st in 38:04 for 10,000 meters.

USTFF Cross-Country at San Diego, CA (11/24/73) – 18:17 for 5000 meters.

1974:

San Diego Relays, CA (4/13/74) – 3rd in mile, 5:04.

PSA-AAU 15K at San Diego, CA (4/20/74) – 1st in 57:22.

Mt. SAC Relays, CA (4/28/74) – ran 2-mile and 3-mile, no times or places available.

Masters meet at Chapman College, CA (5/5/74) – 1st in 34:24 for 6 miles, American track best.

National AAU Women's 10K at New York, NY (5/18/74) – 2nd in 38:03.

Hidden Valley 12-mile, CA (6/15/74) – no time or place available.

Senior Olympics at Irvine, CA (6/22-23/74) – 1500 in 4:54.4, 5000 in 17:59.4.

Semana Nautica 15K at Santa Barbara, CA (7/4/74) – 1st in 1:00:38.

Pierce All-Comers, CA (7/24/74) – mile in 5:05.

Santa Barbara, CA (7/27/74) – 9 miles, 1320 yards in one-hour run.

Pierce All-Comers, CA (8/2/74) – mile in 5:03.5.

Santa Monica, CA (8/18/74) – 1st in 6-mile, 36:42.

Charleston Distance Run, WV (8/31/74) – 2nd in 1:40:50 for 15 miles.

Long Beach Cross-Country, CA (9/14/74) –23:47 for 4 miles.

Florence, Italy (9/29/74) – 1st in 52:15 for 15K, world best.

Long Beach Marathon Prep, CA (10/27/74) – 1:38:58 for 16.2 miles.

SPA-AAU District Cross-Country, CA (11/3/74) – 18:41 for 3.5 miles.

AAU State Cross-Country at San Diego, CA (11/10/74) – 4th in 17:28 for 5000 meters.

No name or location listed for this race (11/17/74) – 59 minutes for 10.09 miles.

1975:

Sunkist Qualifier at Westwood, CA (1/5/75) – mile in 4:52.1.

So-Cal Indoor at Anaheim, CA (1/24/75) – 1st in 2-mile, 10:36.

Lakewood Invitational, CA (5/3/75) – 1st in 5000, 17:28.

Mini-Marathon at New York, NY (5/10/75) – 2nd in 36:04 for 10K.

Bakersfield, CA (5/17/75) – 1st in half-marathon, 1:21.

No name or location listed for this race (5/24/75) – 5000 in 16:55.

SPA-AAU Championships, CA (6/8/75) – 1st in 2-mile, 10:28.0.

San Juan 450, Puerto Rico (6/24/75) – 1st in 2:11:54 for 30K.

National AAU Championships, NJ (1975) – 12th in 9:55 for 3000 meters.

Semana Nautica 15K at Santa Barbara, CA (7/4/75) – 1st in 56:04.

Santa Barbara, CA (7/19/75) – 10 miles, 112 yards for one-hour run.

Santa Barbara CA (7/26/75) – 10 miles, 243 yards for one-hour run.

Griffith Park 13K at Los Angeles, CA (8/2/75) – 1st in 52:13.

Huntington Beach 10-Mile, CA (8/9/75) – 1st in 59:09.

Long Beach Grand Prix 10K, CA (9/27/75) – 2nd in 17:15.

Blue Angels Sports Festival at Fountain Valley, CA (10/4/75) – 3rd in 6:55 for 5K cross-country.

Long Beach Marathon Prep, CA (10/26/75) – 1:36:44 for 16.2 miles.

Alonda Park 4-person 10-mile relay, CA (11/2/75) – 4th leg in about 23 minutes.

SPA-AAU Cross-Country Championships, CA (11/7/75) – 4th place individual, 2nd team.

AAU State Cross-Country Championships, CA (11/16/75) – 5th place individual, 3rd team.

Sao Silvestre at Sao Paulo, Brazil (12/31/75) – 2nd in 29:52 for 8.4K.

1976:

Daisy Hill Run at San Francisco, CA (1/11/76) – 1st in 13.5-mile race.

SPA-AAU 30K at Culver City, CA (2/15/76) – 1st in 1:54:47.

Lunada Bay 25K, CA (3/13/76) – 1st in 1:35:39.

San Diego Cougars Invitational, CA (3/13/76) – 3rd in mile, 5:06.

La Mirada 2-Person 14-mile Relay, CA (4/3/76) – 1:18:25 total time.

Mini-Marathon at New York, NY (5/8/76) – 3rd in 36:03 for 10K.

Exhibition Women's 10,000 meters at Eugene, OR (5/22/76) – 4th in 36:24.

Two-person 10-Mile Relay at Cerritos, CA (7/18/76) – 2nd in total time of 51:40; I averaged 2:33 half-miles.

Harbor Regional Park, CA (9/24/76) – 2nd in 18:14 for 5K cross-country.

10K road race at Steinem, West Germany (10/3/76) – 1st in about 42 minutes.

15K road race at Vienna, Austria (10/23/76) – 55:07.

SPA-AAU Cross-Country, CA (11/7/76) – 1st in 5K.

Laguna Niguel, CA (11/14/76) – 35 minutes, probably short of advertised 10K.

National AAU Cross-Country Championships at Miami, FL (11/27/76) – 3rd place team.

Sao Silvestre at Sao Paulo, Brazil (12/31/76) – 8th in 32:12 for 8.4K (very ill).

1977:

140-mile Perimeter Relay at Honolulu, HI (2/6/77) – averaged 6-minute miles for 7 legs between 1.5 and 4.7 miles.

SPA-AAU Championship 30K at Culver City, CA (2/20/77) – 1st in 2:02.

Lunada Bay 25K, CA (3/12/77) – 1:43:28.

Mini-Marathon 10K at New York, NY (6/4/77) – 23rd in 37:31.

National AAU Championships 10,000 meters at Westwood, CA (6/9/77) – 11th in 36:06

Chicago Distance Classic, IL (7/3/77) – 1:15 for 20K.

1978:

140-mile Perimeter Relay at Honolulu, HI (1/22/78) – ran 7 legs, between 1.4 and 3.4 miles, totaling 18.5 miles.

Hidden Valley 6-mile, CA (1978) – 34:49.

Bonne Bell 10K at Phoenix, AZ (3/4/78) – 5th in 37:00.

Bloomsday Race at Spokane, WA (5/7/78) – 49:03 for 8.25 miles.

Brentwood 10K, CA (5/28/78) – 1st in 35:50.

Mini-Marathon at New York, NY (6/3/78) – 23rd in 37:15 for 10K.

Anne & Mary Days 7.2K at Blue Lake, CA (8/13/78) – 1st in 27:02.

National AAU 50-mile at Santa Monica, CA (9/9/78) – 1st in 7:14:58. Set world records at these intermediate distances: 20K, 1:30:41; 15 miles, 1:48:17; 25K, 1:52:02; 30K, 2:14:04; 20 miles, 2:23:52; 35K, 2:36:50; 40K, 3:00:41; 25 miles, 3:01:50; marathon, 3:11:50; 30 miles, 3:45:47, and 50K, 3:51:01. All but the 50K were a half-mile longer than the listed distance because of a clerical error.

Nike Challenge 15K at Minneapolis, MN (9/16/78) – 7th in 1:00:12.

Freedom Trail Run at Boston, MA (9/30/78) – 10th in 49:24 for 8 miles.

Bonne Bell 10K at Boston, MA (10/9/78) – 25th in 36:53 for 10K.

1979:

SPA-AAU 30K Championships at Culver City, CA (2/18/79) – 1st in 2:09:53.

El Cajon 20K, CA (2/24/79) – 4th in 1:22:00.

Black History Month 10K at Carson, CA (2/24/79) – 2nd in 37:45, 1st 30-plus.

SPA-AAU 25K Championships at Ventura, CA (3/3/79) – 1st in 1:40:13.

Athlete's Foot 10K at Palos Verdes, CA (3/18/79) – tied for 1st with Gayle Barron.

George Allen March of Dimes 10K at Palos Verdes, CA (4/21/79) – 3rd in 38:28.

Palos Verdes Library 10K, CA (9/15/79) – 1st in 37:26.

1981 (none in 1980):

Topanga 10K, CA (5/23/81) – 1st in 43:44, trail run.

Brentwood 10K, CA (5/24/81) – 3rd in 37:33.

1982:

Oregon Track Club 30K at Eugene, OR (8/1/82) – 1st in 1:58:34, long course.

Nike High Altitude Challenge at Boulder, CO (9/12/82) – 3rd in 37:45 for 10K.

Dannon 10K at Eugene, OR (11/6/82) – 3rd in 35:32.

1983:

Amish County Half-Marathon at Lancaster, PA (4/17/83) – 3rd in 1:22:45.

Oregon Track Club Women's 10K at Eugene, OR (5/1/83) – 6th in 37:31.

Viking Classic 8K at Portland, OR (5/22/83) – 2nd in 29:08.

Alaska Women's 10K at Anchorage, AK (6/11/83) – 2nd in 37:08.

1984:

SPA-TAC Championship 5K at Westlake, CA (3/25/84) – 3rd in 17:44, 1st 30-plus.

Malibu 10K, CA (4/7/84) – 36:51.

Michigan City 15K, IN (5/20/84) – 2nd in 55:34, 1st in 35-39 division.

Basin Blues Hansen Dam 10-mile at Sylmar, CA (6/3/84) – 2nd in 1:02:15, 1st in 35-plus.

1985:

Mini-Marathon at New York, NY (6/1/85) – 40:30 for 10K.

1987 (none in 1986):

National Masters Track and Field at Eugene, OR (1987) – 1st in 5000 meters, 35-39 division.

World Veterans Games at Melbourne, Australia (1987) – 1st in 35-39 division 1500 meters, 4:42.0; 1st in 35-39 division 5000 meters, 17:43.1.

Training in Peak Years

I kept 40 years worth of journals, logging nearly every workout and race I ran from my first year of college on. My training under Laszlo Tabori began in late 1970-early 1971. Of all the years, it is apparent to me that 1974 and 1975 produced my best performances, as they were topped by two marathon world records.

We ran in those two years at Valley College in the city of Van Nuys, California. It was a dirt track of 440 yards, with a grass infield and surrounded by grass athletic fields. I estimate that the warm-up loops we ran on those fields were 1000 meters around the perimeter (a bit longer than a half-mile). All the rest of the workout was conducted on that track.

We met there every Tuesday and Thursday at 5 P.M. and quite often on Saturday afternoons at 2:30. Even on the track, Laszlo made the distinction between running on the dirt track for the hard efforts and on the grass infield for the recovery running and all the distances he wasn't timing.

1974 WORKOUTS

By the beginning of 1974, I was decidedly a marathoner but still training like a 1500-meter runner, doing intervals on the track under Coach Laszlo's strict rule at least three times a week. The difference, at least to my mind, was that the volume of intervals increased, and so did my mileage on the in-between days on the roads.

The fact that I was running on the roads at all was a marked change, considering that in my first year with him our feet never touched pavement. This all changed after I won Boston in 1973.

Laszlo and I were learning together how to be and coach a road runner. We had our disagreements along the way, like drinking Gookinaid (ERG) during workouts. I hid it in the women's restroom for me and my teammates, and he was mighty angry about that when he discovered the drink.

I also learned about hydration and fueling through nutrition, and about lightweight shoes, shorts and shirts. Remember, this was an era before digital watches, Gu or gels, replacement drinks (other than Gookinaid), uniform material that "wicked" and breathed, and running bras. This was a time before the term "sports psychology" existed. I prepared intuitively and instinctively, and sometimes I got it right.

January 1974 opened with a traditional New Year's run to "three trees," a local runners' loop from Cal-State Northridge to the peak in the foothills north of campus, Mission Peak, marked by oak trees – thus the nickname. It was a 19-mile run round-trip, and you proved you made it up there if you discovered the secret of the nickname (which I will not reveal here). I ran with my teammate Judy Graham and a visiting runner from Kansas, Teri Anderson.

Teri was a nationally ranked collegiate miler, and being from the flat plains of Kansas she did not appreciate the trail run up the "mountain" one bit. She said it was not for runners; it was for mountain goats. I thought I was taking her on one of my pride and joy courses, but she was not appreciative. Since we ended up walking most of it, the run was ruined, so I returned to do it by myself later.

I averaged about 85 miles per week in January. Then February was injury-ridden with back problems, so the mileage went down and my indoor track season went with it. The back problem was due to a well-intended but ill-advised decision to take a body-conditioning class at school.

I rebounded fine in March with mileage up over 400 miles for the month. April was another good month with more than 400 miles and some good racing on the track. But the payoff came in May when I set an American best mark in a six-mile race on the track, with 34:24. May ended in about 300 miles, a head cold and a slow start for the month of June. I summed up the first half of the year in my journal:

After my back injury, there followed eight weeks of high mileage, averaging up to 98.5 miles per week and then the six-mile record... only to result in another infection, illness and a cold. Does this say anything about over-training?

June was a more consistent month of training, with a few races, and overall mileage about 250 miles. I raced on the roads in July, keeping the mileage strong at about 300 and was healthy overall. I was still training with Laszlo, but in the summer on his vacation I sometimes accompanied Tom Sturak at his workouts with Joe Douglas and the Santa Monica Track Club. August was similar, with the highest week peaking at 122 miles.

My longest single training run leading up to my next marathon was 22 miles. All year long, I ran double workouts the majority of weekdays, the morning run usually being short and the evening run usually long interval workouts.

A good part of September and October were spent in Europe, so the daily mileage is a little vague.

September totaled about 318 miles, and October was about 250 miles. The trip produced some of my best racing to date (notably my first sub-three-hour marathon in West Germany and a 15K world record in Italy), which was more valuable than any training. Who said "you learn to race by racing"? Wise.

I returned home to more intervals and to cross-country races, with November at 374 miles and December at 331 miles. The year ended with a grand total of 3882 miles. Most importantly, I was rewarded with another PR marathon and my first world record by year's end – 2:43:54 at the Western Hemisphere Marathon in Culver City.

(For details of daily training for the entire year of 1974, refer to my web page at:
http://www.jacquelinehansen.com/coaching)

1975 TRAINING

Although I closed out the previous year with a marathon, I returned to the track with strong (and long) interval workouts in 1975. Laszlo kept us on an annual schedule of winter indoor track, spring outdoor track, summer base-laying mileage with some vacation and fall cross-country. I was adding the dimension of road running, and it seemed to fit best into the fall season most of the time.

I salvaged a better indoor season in 1975, starting in January with a mile time-trial on New Year's Day and a qualifying race at UCLA to gain entry to the Sunkist Indoor Meet. I ran strong interval workouts and seemed primed for a good track season. Unfortunately, the first meet of the year, at Sunkist, ended in a big collision on the track. My back suffered another injury when I went down on the track and was stepped on by the other runners – with spikes – going over the small of my back.

January ended with 247 miles, February at 284 miles, and then March, April and May all rebounded closer to 400 miles again. I ran a combination of track and road races, including a good 10K performance at the New York Mini and a half-marathon in California. On the track, I ran well at the mile, the two-mile and 5000-meter distances.

What was not so well done, I went abroad to race a 30K road race in Puerto Rico less than a week before my national track 3000 meters, and the latter race suffered the consequences.

The summer months, June, July and August, were all close to 400 miles each. I ran more road races, but the best performances came running on the track – in the one-hour run. I competed in it twice in back-to-back weeks and went more than 10 miles both times.

I seemed to run better marathons in the fall, in great part because the longer, sunnier summer days lent themselves to better, more consistent training. I think back to training for Boston 1973 in the short winter days, and I remember that 11 out of my 13 weekly workouts were run in the dark (before school in the morning and after work at night). That was the biggest challenge to overcome.

The fall season of 1975 produced my all-time peak marathon. The proof is in the pudding, it is said, and my "pudding" was a workout that convinced Laszlo I was ready. It came in September, another 400-mile month. The key workout came on the last day of that month.

Note: the timed efforts were run on the dirt track, and the rest on the grass on the infield, paralleling lane one. The mile time-trials were part of a five-lap set, and you never knew which four laps were being timed, so you ran all five hard. Not shown are the recovery walk-jogs done between the distances, but these are included in the overall total mileage. (For example, we might get a whole 440 jog for each 440 effort, but recovery time varied.)

2½-mile warm-up
15 x 100 (8 medium, 7 hard)
10 x 440 (#3-6-9 hard in 73, 71, 72 seconds)
2½ laps easy
8 x 150 (2 medium + 2 hard & repeat)
5 laps hard (4-lap mile in 5:13)
8 x 150 (2 medium + 1 hard & repeat; last 2 medium)
2 laps easy
5 laps hard (4-lap mile in 5:17)
2½ laps easy
10 x 220 (2 medium +1 hard & repeat; last 2 medium)

This workout lasted three hours and totaled 18 miles. A week later, I departed for Eugene, Oregon. On October 12, I ran the Nike-OTC Marathon, breaking 2:40 (with 2:38:19) for the first time by any woman.

Returning home from Eugene, I joined my team and finished the year with cross-country meets and road races, and one more marathon. I maintained monthly mileage of 300 to 400, and stayed injury- and illness-free through December.

The year ended with 4142 total miles. I was pleased to win the Honolulu Marathon in course-record time and followed that performance by running in the Sao Silvestre race in Brazil on New Year's Eve. It is no wonder I refer to 1974 and 1975 as my peak years.

(For details of daily training for the entire year of 1975, refer to my web page at: http://www.jacquelinehansen.com/coaching)

Training with Leal-Ann Reinhart in the late 1970s.

History Repeated

Living a parallel existence nearly three decades apart, women ski jumpers have something in common with women distance runners. Obviously, the commonalities are not the physical aspects of their events; they could not be more different. But both sets of athletes know what it's like to be discriminated against by their international governing bodies.

Both know what it's like to watch an Olympics (or two or three) go by without an opportunity to compete, no matter if you're the best in the world. Both wondered if they would have an Olympic opportunity in their relatively short athletic lifetimes.

Back in 2005, at the LA84 Foundation, we honored a young, outstanding ski jumper, Abby Hughes, at our National Women and Girls in Sports Day awards luncheon. She was very shy and modest, but in her few words she spoke volumes by stating that she wished she would be allowed to ski jump in the Olympics. My heart went out to her on the spot. Those words echoed my own back in 1974 after my first marathon world record, and again in 1975 after my second record.

As a 1500-meter runner, I would have had a clear path of opportunity available to me that led from a national championships, to an Olympic Trials and onto the Olympic team. In reality, this only occurred as of 1972. It was shocking to me at the time that this was the latest and longest event available to women runners.

I thought then that the situation could be remedied with lobbying, a letter-writing campaign or a petition-signing drive. I was naive beyond imagination. It was not to be, and the 1976 Montreal Olympic Games passed me by.

In 1979, my husband and I were founding members of an organization called the International Runners Committee, sponsored by Nike, created for lobbying purposes to seek the inclusion of the marathon, 5000- and 10,000-meter events into the Olympic Games. The fight was long and hard, and ultimately successful.

In 2006, the vice-president of the Women's Ski Jumping Foundation, Peter Jerome, walked into the LA84 Foundation, seeking advice and hopefully support for his daughter and her teammates to move their event forward onto the Olympic scene. He met with the president of LA84, Anita De Frantz, due to her position within the Olympic Committee.

She then introduced him to me as the person who had navigated this path before. I shared with him the story of how the women's distance events came into the Olympic Games, and about our battle for the marathon, 5000- and 10,000-meter races. I told him about the international class-action lawsuit against the IOC and related entities.

A year later, in September 2007, I was a guest in Park City, Utah, to witness an international competition of women ski jumpers – and, surprisingly to me, without snow. This suited me perfectly. I favor fine-weather competition like the Southern California climate I come from.

I tried to describe to my incredulous running friends that competitors can ski jump in warm weather on a hill covered with what looks like hundreds of hula skirts laid out in overlapping patterns, like shingles on a roof.

216

I made sure to experience every vantage point – from the bottom, side and top. I sat on the pole the jumpers launch themselves from, and it seemed to me like launching yourself out of an airplane. I watched from the sides, where the judges stand and could see jumpers literally in flight. I watched near that point where the coaches stand as athletes fly overhead. I watched from the bottom to see the incredible landings, where one fall could end a career. This sport requires helmets and padded gear for good reasons. My admiration for the jumpers grew. They are courageous and brave athletes, and they deserved the world stage.

In Park City, Peter Jerome introduced me to Deedee Corradini, former mayor of Salt Lake City who was instrumental in gaining the Winter Olympics for Utah in 2002. As president of the Women's Ski Jumping Foundation, she spearheaded the women's movement to gain inclusion in the Olympics. I gave interviews to the press on the jumpers' behalf.

Lindsey Van, 2010 world ski jumping champion, had been working toward the Olympics since she was 12. She had been the point person among the athletes in the court case against the IOC – all the while leading the way by her example.

In February 2011, as defending champion, Lindsey did not make it to the finals in the World Championships. The weather was horrific, but all the women participated in solidarity, and their efforts sealed the fact that they were prepared to compete at the highest levels, whatever it took. Deedee Corradini described the importance of that event for the NPR program "Only a Game." She painted the most comprehensive overview of the struggle, its meaning and what lay ahead.

217

On April 6, 2011, the women ski jumpers finally received their long overdue award of Olympic status for the 2014 Games in Sochi, Russia. It had taken nearly seven years of battling, including a lawsuit against the International Olympic Committee, to claim this great victory.

As I reflect on distance runners and ski jumpers, many parallels come to mind. Throughout the ski jumping efforts, I felt at once elated to be involved and to assist, but deeply saddened by the fact that more than 25 years after the women runners' case, discrimination continued. The IOC dragged its feet as long as possible, denying these women the opportunity of competing in the 2010 Vancouver Games.

With Abby Hughes in 2006 at Park City, Utah.

This I Believe

In 2009, I felt compelled to contribute one of those essays solicited by NPR radio for the program "This I Believe." Mine was titled "I Believe in Justice" – for women in sports. I struggle to remember exactly what emotions I felt at the time. Was it outrage, sadness, depression, anger, all of the above, what?

I do know that from the time of the first world record I broke in 1974, I realized the inequity of women's and men's running events in the Olympic Games. I didn't yet realize how big a battle lay ahead or how long the battle would take – approximately a decade!

My essay:

I believe in justice. And I believe in women's rights. I believe women should enjoy the same freedoms men have, such as sports.

When growing up, I was fortunate to have a high school coach who asked why girls weren't allowed to run track like the boys. She initiated the first track and field team for girls at my school. I was a happy participant of the team. Little did I know how that coach's actions would shape my life.

We runners were limited as to how many events and how far we could run. I now know that for decades before me, women all over the world had been deprived the simple freedom to run. In the 1928 Olympic Games at Amsterdam, women gained five track and field events for the first time.

The longest run was only 800 meters, and the three medalists finished faster than the existing world record. Some reporters misrepresented the event to report five women collapsed and five did not even finish. The fact was that nine women finished, running hard – like the men, with only signs of normal fatigue and defeat.

Athletic administrators used the idea of women looking "unwomanly" because of their exertion to stymie their participation in distance races for decades. The 800-meter race was eliminated from the Olympic program until 1960. Longer races were added at a rate likened to "glacial movement." It took until 1972 to add 1500 meters – the "metric mile" – to the Games. It would take until 1984 to add the 3000 meters.

In between those years, women's running gained immense popularity around the world. From cross-country distance races of two miles to 10 kilometers, women of all ages were competing in schools, universities and clubs and on their own. They were running road races, from five kilometers to marathons, by the thousands.

However, they were not running in the Olympic Games. There were a few women who questioned that blatant omission. Like my high school coach who asked why we girls were not allowed to run, I am proud to have been among those who questioned why, or more importantly, "Why not?" The turbulent 1960s were known for questioning authority.

Becoming an activist during the 1970s feminist movement was a natural transition for me. In 1977, I attended a national women's conference to seek support for my newfound cause to put women's running on the international scene. Humbled by all women's causes that seemed so much more important, I felt there were more life-and-death issues than running.

221

But pushing through those misgivings with the determination of the marathoner I was, I moved forward with efforts to push the boundaries and open the way for women distance runners to compete in the Olympic Games and other international competitions. My colleagues and I formed an international lobbying group known as the International Runners Committee, and the fight was on.

In the end, a women's marathon was successfully lobbied into the 1984 Olympic Games in Los Angeles, through the efforts of not only our organization but those of many individuals worldwide. Other distance events, the 5000 meters and 10,000 meters followed in subsequent Games, but not without an international class-action lawsuit we brought against the governing powers-that-be.

Joan Benoit ran victorious into the L.A. Coliseum and into the history books as the first-ever women's Olympic marathon champion. She was an inspiration to young women all over the world. She led the way and left no doubt that the answer was "yes" to the question whether or not women could endure the distance. Young women all over the world watched her, knowing they too could run after their Olympic dreams.

Coming Next

Special thanks to Joe Henderson and Janet Heinonen for our shared experience in this entire journey, for we share more than "JH" initials and friendship. We have shared a great piece of running history. Joe and Janet not only recorded and guided all the activity of the International Runners Committee, but in the broader picture of our sport we all have them to thank for their contributions recording our running history in its most critical years of development.

Janet and I are working on a book detailing the social and political dimensions behind women's long distance running, from ancient Greece through a 1984 lawsuit by women runners worldwide demanding the International Olympic Committee to add women's distance races on the track. The book title is *Our Longest Run: The History of Women's Long Distance Running.*

We three J.H.'s – Janet, Joe and Jacqueline.

55774898R00125

Made in the USA
Lexington, KY
03 October 2016